Nutri Ninja® | Ninja® Blender System
with Auto-iQ™ Technology

simply DELICIOUS,
simply NUTRITIOUS

150+ DELICIOUS RECIPES

©2014, Euro-Pro Operating, LLC.

All rights reserved. No portion of this book may be reproduced by any means whatsoever without written permission from Euro-Pro Operating, LLC, except for the inclusion of quotations in a media review.

Although every precaution has been taken in the preparation of this book, the publisher and authors assume no responsibility for errors or omissions. Nor is there any liability assumed for damages resulting from the use of the information contained herein. Although every effort has been made to ensure that the information contained in this book is complete and accurate, neither the publisher nor the authors are engaged in rendering professional advice or services to the individual reader. This information is not intended to replace the advice of a medical practitioner, and consumers should always consult with a health care professional prior to making changes to diet or lifestyle, including any new health-related eating programs. Neither the publisher nor author shall be held responsible for any loss or damage allegedly arising from any information or suggestion in this book. The opinions expressed in this book represent the personal views of the authors and not that of the publisher.

Nutritional Analyses: Calculations for the nutritional analyses in this book are based on the largest number of servings listed within the recipes. Calculations are rounded up to the nearest gram or milligram, as appropriate. If two options for an ingredient are listed, the first one is used. Not included are optional ingredients or serving suggestions.

Editors: Mona Wetter Dolgov and Bob Warden
Graphic Designer: Leslie Anne Feagley
Creative Director: Anne Sommers Welch
Photography: Quentin Bacon
Additional Photography: Gary Sloan, Albie Colatonio and Heath Robbins
Food Stylist: Mariana Velasquez
Recipe Development: Euro-Pro Test Kitchen Team Katie Barry, Amy Golino, Vanessa Spillios, and from Great Flavors Test Kitchen: Stephen Delaney, Andrea Schwob, and Bob Warden

Published in the United States of America by
Great Flavors LLC
New Hope, PA 18938

ISBN: 978-1-4951-1607-0

10   9   8   7

Printed in China

table of contents

Watermelon Basil Sangria, page 173

simple, delicious & nutritious

One easy step to transform to a healthier lifestyle is to add more fruits, vegetables, nuts, and seeds into your diet. The Small 18-ounce, Regular 24-ounce, and Jumbo Multi-Serve 32-ounce cups with Auto-iQ™ are YOUR tools to release the amazing power hidden within these essential foods. The powerful Nutri Ninja® high-speed blade system unlocks these fiber-rich foods, turning them into delicious silky-smooth, grit-free nutrient extractions. The Auto-iQ™ Nutri Ninja® BLEND and ULTRA BLEND programs allow you to make these nutrient-rich drinks automatically at the touch of a button. With the Nutri Ninja® cups, you can also make homemade, preservative-free salad dressings, vegetable dips, and fresh fruit desserts.

Cup Conversion

To convert a Small 18-ounce Cup recipe to a Jumbo Multi-Serve 32-ounce one, multiply ingredients by 2. To convert a Regular 24-ounce Cup recipe to a Jumbo Multi-Serve 32-ounce Cup multiply by 1.5.

In the large 72-ounce Pitcher, touch the Auto-iQ™ FROZEN DRINKS/ SMOOTHIES button to create family smoothies and frozen cocktails. Use the Auto-iQ™ PUREE button to turn fresh vegetables, herbs, and beans into silky-smooth vegetable purees, soups, dips, and more!

In the 56-ounce Food Processor Bowl, use Auto-iQ™ PULSE to prepare perfectly chopped vegetables, meats and more. Every pulse is precisely pulsed so there is no guesswork and no over-processing. Auto-iQ™ PULSE chops any vegetable, fruit, meat, or beans to any desired consistency, from dice to mince. You can even make a restaurant quality chopped salad!

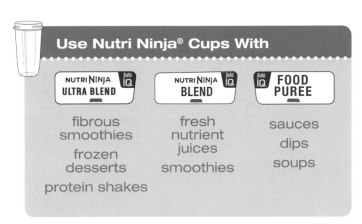

Use Nutri Ninja® Cups With

NUTRI NINJA ULTRA BLEND (Auto iQ)	NUTRI NINJA BLEND (Auto iQ)	(Auto iQ) FOOD PUREE
fibrous smoothies	fresh nutrient juices	sauces
frozen desserts	smoothies	dips
protein shakes		soups

Use Pitcher With

(Auto iQ) FROZEN DRINKS SMOOTHIES	(Auto iQ) FOOD PUREE
cocktails	sauces
smoothies	dips
frozen desserts	soups
milkshakes	

why nutrient extract?

Nutrient extract juices provide you with a simple way to boost your daily recommended nutritional intake. Key benefits include:

- Slower absorption of nutrients vs. juicing—more continual energy source
- Good source of nutrition—easy way to get your daily servings of fruits and vegetables
- Great variety of ingredients, textures, and flavor options
- Can be a quick and easy meal replacement
- Easy additions of protein and "good fats"
- Adds fiber to your diet

wellness categories

We've outlined five of the top wellness categories and created recipes to help you on your journey toward optimal health.

Detox/Cleanse

Your body has an internal detoxification system that involves several major organs, including the liver and kidneys. Choose the following beneficial super-food boosters:

- A digestive aid, **lemon** can help your liver enzymes work overtime.
- Fresh herbs, such as **ginger** and **mint,** ramp up flavor while providing antioxidants.
- **Cilantro** and **parsley** are flavorful, and the ultimate herbal detoxifiers.
- Cruciferous vegetables, such as **kale, broccoli,** and **cabbage,** contain detoxifying sulfur.

Heart Health

Making certain that your heart is in tip-top shape is key to living well. Be sure to include foods that support your heart and circulation, along with exercise and other stress reduction techniques.

- **Berries** are antioxidant powerhouses that can help control inflammation, a heart disease risk factor.
- **Ground flaxseed** or **flax oil** can help maintain cholesterol levels within already normal ranges.
- A good source of plant protein, **walnuts** contain beneficial omega-3 fats.
- **Avocados,** packed with monounsaturated fats, can help maintain appropriate blood fat levels.

Longevity + Beauty

Looking good and living a healthy life can be supported by being mindful of the right food choices. A variety of foods can bolster your immune system and support detoxification to get you on your way to a long and beautiful life.

- **Lemons** and **limes** help improve the body's alkalinity, a positive step for radiant skin.
- **Avocados** and **coconut oil** provide an excellent dose of healthy fats to help your skin look its best.
- A good source of vitamins A, C, and calcium, **arugula** can help protect your skin from free radicals.
- High in antioxidants, **green tea** is a well-known life enhancer in many cultures.

Weight Loss Wellness

Jump-start your weight and fitness efforts by simply adding one of our green-based smoothies or juices to your food plan.

- To keep your blood sugar steady, within already normal levels, select mostly low-sugar fruits, such as **berries, lemons,** and **limes.**
- Teas such as **roobois** and **green** are zero-calorie, flavorful ways to bump up your antioxidant intake.
- Seeds such as **chia** and **sunflower** thicken smoothies, boost nutrients, and help you feel full.
- Lacto-fermented foods, such as **kimchi** and **kombucha,** provide good bacteria, improving digestion with soluble and insoluble fibers that help your regularity.

Mood + Immunity

The gut is often called the second brain because about 85% of neurotransmitters are produced in the GI tract.

- B vitamins, which abound in **dark leafy greens,** help regulate bodily processes and balance mood.
- **Coconut water** adds potassium and other electrolytes, which help keep you hydrated.
- An herb that adapts to your stress level, **holy basil,** or **tulsi,** is available in tea bags.
- **Tart cherry juice concentrate** is a premier ingredient to help support the immune system.

Power Ball, page 71

7

is organic important?

Vegetables, fruits, and food grown organically or without the use of potentially harmful pesticides may contain more nutrients than "conventionally grown" produce. To help you select organic produce with the least amount of pesticides, the Environmental Working Group compiles a yearly list of the Dirty Dozen Plus™ and Clean 15™. To learn more about the EWG, the Dirty Dozen Plus™ and Clean 15™ classifications, and find the most up-to-date EWG lists, visit **www.ewg.org.**

Dirty Dozen Plus™

- apples
- celery
- cherry tomatoes
- collard greens
- cucumbers
- grapes
- hot peppers
- kale
- nectarines
- peaches
- potatoes
- spinach
- strawberries
- sweet bell peppers
- zucchini

The Clean 15™

- asparagus
- avocados
- cabbage
- cantaloupe
- eggplant
- grapefruit
- kiwi
- mangoes
- mushrooms
- onions
- papayas
- pineapple
- sweet corn
- sweet peas, frozen
- sweet potatoes
- watermelon

pantry list to get started

Here is a list of all the key ingredients for the recipes in this book to help you get started with your shopping list!

Pantry List

sweeteners
agave nectar
coconut palm sugar
honey
pitted dates
pure maple syrup
raisins
stevia

fresh/frozen fruits
acai berry puree
apple
avocado
banana
blueberries
dark sweet cherries
frozen fruits
green and red grapes
kiwi
lemon
lime
mango
mixed berries
orange
papaya
passion fruit pulp
peach
pear
pineapple
raspberries
rhubarb

strawberry
tomato
watermelon

vegetables
alfalfa sprouts
baby arugula
baby spinach
beets
carrot
celery
cucumber
kale
red and green cabbage
red leaf lettuce
romaine lettuce
sweet potato

milks, juices & waters
carrot juice
coconut water
flax milk, original flavor
kombucha, original flavor
lemonade
oat milk, vanilla flavor
pomegranate juice
rice milk, original flavor
skim and whole milk
unsweetened apple juice

unsweetened coconut milk
unsweetened vanilla
   almond milk

seasonings
cardamom powder
celery seed
cocoa powder
fresh basil
fresh ginger
fresh mint
green curry paste
ground cinnamon
ground nutmeg
hot sauce
pumpkin pie spice
pure vanilla extract
rose water
tamarind concentrate

nuts, seeds & butters
almonds
almond butter
cashew butter
chia seeds
ground flaxseeds
peanut butter
pumpkin seeds
sesame seeds

shelled hemp seeds
sunflower butter
sunflower seeds
walnuts

forward thinking
acai powder
aloe vera juice
bee pollen
cacao nibs
cacao powder
coconut oil
flaxseed oil
holy basil powder
maca powder
nutritional yeast
spirulina
tart cherry juice
   concentrate

other
goji berries
pumpkin puree
quick rolled oats
quinoa
soft and firm tofu

nature's super-food ingredients

These bonus ingredients can add great flavor and bump up nutritional value to your nutrient-rich juices. Look for these ingredients as you explore new recipes in this book!

Bonus Ingredient	Characteristics
Acai	• Unique, complex blend of essential fats, antioxidants, amino acids, and calcium • Available in powder and frozen concentrate; has a berry flavor without sweetness
Aloe Vera Juice	• Can serve as a way of cleansing the body of toxins • Features a bright, refreshing flavor
Basil	• Contains micronutrients, such as manganese and copper, providing antioxidant properties • Fragrant, large-leaf herb tastes great with other greens and strawberries
Chia Seeds	• A total package with protein, fiber, calcium, and omega-3 fats that can help with regularity and weight management • Easily absorbs liquids, making drinks thicker, with a slightly nutty taste
Cilantro	• An excellent detoxifier that binds heavy metals, helping to eliminate toxins from the body • Delicate leaf herb that pairs well with vegetables and fruits including avocado and tomato
Cinnamon	• Pairs well with nut milks, raisins, dates, and winter fruits and vegetable
Coconut Oil	• Contains medium-chain triglycerides, which can promote the burning of fat • Adds a smoothness to blended drinks and keeps you feeling full
Flaxseeds	• Contain lignans, a class of phytoestrogens considered to have antioxidant properties • Grind seeds well to release nutrients or use ground flax; store in the refrigerator after grinding or opening
Ginger	• An anti-inflammatory plant root that can aid the immune system and help quell nausea

Bonus Ingredient	Characteristics
Goji Berries	• A concentrated source of amino acids and antioxidants that may help support the immune system • Provide a hint of sweetness and texture to food; available as dried berries
Hemp Seeds	• Packed with protein, iron, and vitamin E • The slightly nutty flavor goes well with vegetables or fruits
Maca	• An adaptogen that can regulate mood and energy levels, and support a healthy libido • Expect a bland cocoa flavor with a hint of sweetness
Mint	• An herb that promotes beneficial enzymes that can help soothe the digestive tract • Has a cool minty flavor that complements several types of fruits
Parsley	• Offers great antioxidant support and high in flavonoids and vitamin A and C • Not only a garnish, it's a great additive for green drinks
Pomegranate Juice	• A triple play of antioxidants—anthocyanins, tannins, ellagic acid—for immune and blood pressure support • Intensely flavored as a juice or concentrate; pairs well with berries and chocolate
Turmeric	• Contains curcumin, an active component that supports joint health and cardiovascular function • Pairs well with carrots, sweet potatoes
Tart Cherry Juice	• Contains phytonutrients that help reduce inflammation, aid in exercise recovery, and improve sleep

sugar & fiber in fruits & vegetables

The sugar and fiber content of fruits and vegetables can be helpful when deciding which foods to use in your drinks, particularly if you're concerned about weight loss. The following charts reflect the fruits and vegetables used in our recipes. Listed according to sugar content, from lowest to highest value, the following charts also provide the corresponding fiber content. The values indicated are for typical serving sizes of each food. For items indicating "1" piece, the fruits are medium in size.

Try to avoid added sugars in your diet, which are found in processed foods. Instead, get your sugar from naturally occurring sources, such as fruits and vegetables. Along with natural sugar, nature packages fruits and vegetables with fiber, vitamins, minerals, and antioxidants— what you need for vibrant health.

Low Sugar Content Foods

FOOD	SERVING SIZE	SUGAR (GRAMS)	FIBER (GRAMS)
Cilantro	1 cup	0	1
Spinach	1 cup	0	1
Dandelion greens	1 cup	0	2
Swiss chard	1 cup	0	1
Romaine	1 cup	1	1
Watercress	1 cup	1	0
Parsley	1 cup	1	2
Celery	1	1	1
Bok choy	1 cup	1	1
Kale	1 cup	1	2
Lime	1 cup	1	2
Avocado	1 cup	1	10
Kiwi	1	2	6
Lemon	1	2	2
Cabbage	1 cup	3	2
Goji berries	2 tbsp.	4	1
Tomato	1 cup	5	2
Coconut	1 cup	5	7
Pepper	1	5	3
Raspberries	1 cup	5	8

High Sugar Content Foods

FOOD	SERVING SIZE	SUGAR (GRAMS)	FIBER (GRAMS)
Nectarine	1	11	2
Orange	1	12	3
Peach	1	12	2
Cantaloupe	1 cup	13	1
Honeydew	1 cup	14	1
Banana	1	14	3
Blueberries	1 cup	15	4
Grapes	1 cup	15	1
Pineapple	1 cup	16	2
Fig	2	16	3
Pear	1	17	6
Apple	1	19	4
Mango	1 cup	23	3
Date	2	32	3

Moderate Sugar Content Foods

FOOD	SERVING SIZE	SUGAR (GRAMS)	FIBER (GRAMS)
Sweet potato	1 cup	6	4
Blackberries	1 cup	7	8
Strawberries	1 cup	7	3
Beets	1 cup	9	4
Grapefruit	1	9	1
Tangerine	1	9	2
Watermelon	1 cup	9	1

customize your own...

Get creative with your Nutri Ninja®, and customize a healthy blend of your very own! Don't be afraid to experiment. Check out our suggestions below for creating your own signature nutrient extract juice!

To Make It Thicker

Try adding one of these ingredients for a creamier drink and to boost your nutritional intake:

- ¼ ripe banana
- 2 tablespoons avocado
- ½ tablespoon chia seeds

HOW TO MAKE A CHIA GEL: Combine 4 tablespoons of chia seeds with 2 cups of water or another liquid like coconut water. After 10 to 15 minutes, you'll have a gel! Use 1 or 2 tablespoons of gel to thicken drinks to your desired consistency. Cover and refrigerate for up to 1 week.

To Make It Thinner

The thickness of blended drinks depends on ice usage and whether the ingredients are fresh or frozen. To regulate the consistency of your smoothies and beverages, you can add one of these healthful ingredients to thin it down:

- 2 tablespoons green tea or chamomile tea
- 2 tablespoons coconut water
- Add a small amount of a high-moisture food, such as celery, lettuce, cucumber, lemon, or lime
- Add water—important to rehydrate!
- Unsweetened almond milk adds richness, great with tropical fruits!

The recipes in this book are created with ingredients that are naturally low in sugar. If your taste buds require beverages that are a little sweeter, we recommend using the ingredients in the chart below.

To Make It Sweeter

SWEETENER	AMOUNTS	CALORIES	CHARACTERISTICS
Agave	1 tsp.	20	• Sourced from the root of the agave or yucca plant.
Dates	½ date	30	• Dried fruits provide very concentrated, natural sweetness.
Dried Figs	½ fig	30	• Dried fruits provide very concentrated, natural sweetness.
Raisins	20 raisins	30	• Dried fruits provide very concentrated, natural sweetness.
Honey	1½ tsp.	32	• Distinct rich taste—opt for raw organic honey.
Lucuma	1½ tsp.	30	• A subtropical fruit available in powder form found in most health food stores. • Fragrant, sweet, and emulsifies fats if blended.
Maple Syrup	1½ tsp.	25	• Obtained from the sap of the maple tree. • Concentrated sweetness.
Stevia	½ packet	0	• An herb available in powdered or liquid form with zero calories. • Several brands of Stevia may have a slight taste difference because they are harvested from different parts of the plant.
Yacon Syrup	1½ tsp.	20	• Sourced from a South American tuber. Also available in powdered form. Sold at health food stores. • Offers half the calories of table sugar.

mix & match recipe ideas

Create your own nutrient-rich juices, smoothies, soups, dips, and sauces with these great food and flavor combos!

These Taste Great	With Any of These
apples, pears, nut milks	cinnamon, nutmeg, almonds, walnuts
kale, Swiss chard, romaine	fresh lemons, pears, kiwi, ginger
green tea	all berries, tart cherry and pomegranate concentrates
sweet potatoes, carrots, butternut squash	turmeric, maple syrup
arugula	mint, pears, apples
pineapple, mango, papaya	coconut, bananas
strawberries	basil, mint, goji berries

Kale & Sunflower Pesto, page 112

powerhouse combinations

Sometimes using ingredients together delivers a bigger nutritional benefit than consuming them individually. Here are a few go-together ideas for creating your own drinks that will complement your healthy eating efforts.

- **Citrus + dark leafy greens =**
  Optimal absorption of the iron in greens with the help of vitamin C–rich citrus

- **Kale or Swiss chard + strawberries =**
  Higher availability of B vitamins found in leafy greens along with the vitamin C in berries

- **Sweet potatoes or carrots + nuts =**
  Improved absorption of fat-soluble vitamin A, contained in many orange foods, possible with the help of the healthy fats in nuts

- **Full-fat coconut milk or coconut oil + turmeric =**
  Better utilization of turmeric's potent antioxidant compound, curcumin, aided by the fat in coconut

- **Avocado or nuts + tomatoes or watermelon =**
  Enhanced absorption of lycopene—the red-colored antioxidant—with the assistance of the healthy fats in avocado or nuts

healthy swaps

Use this guide for entrées, soups, sides, and baked goods to make your meals even healthier!

Healthy Swaps

	INSTEAD OF	SUBSTITUTE THIS
DAIRY	Sour cream	Plain low-fat yogurt
	Milk, evaporated	Evaporated skim milk
	Whole milk	Fat-free milk
	Cheddar cheese	Low-fat Cheddar cheese
	Ice cream	Frozen yogurt or sorbet
	Cream cheese	Neufchâtel or light cream cheese
	Whipped cream	Light whipped topping
	Ricotta cheese	Low-fat ricotta cheese
	Cream	Fat-free half-and-half, evaporated skim milk
	Yogurt, fruit-flavored	Plain yogurt with fresh fruit slices
	Sour cream, full-fat	Fat-free/low-fat sour cream, plain fat-free/low-fat yogurt
PROTEIN	Bacon	Canadian bacon, turkey bacon, smoked turkey, or lean prosciutto (Italian ham)
	Ground beef	Extra-lean or lean ground beef, skinless chicken or turkey breast, tofu, tempeh
	Meat as the main ingredient	Three times as many vegetables as the meat on pizzas or in casseroles, soups, and stews
	Eggs	Two egg whites or ¼ cup egg substitute for each whole egg
OTHER	Soups, creamed	Fat-free milk-based soups, mashed potato flakes, or pureed carrots, potatoes, or tofu for thickening agents
	Soups, sauces, dressings, crackers, or canned meat, fish, or vegetables	Low-sodium or reduced-sodium versions

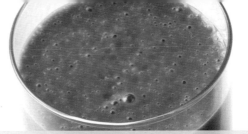

Healthy Swaps

	INSTEAD OF	SUBSTITUTE THIS
GRAINS	Bread, white Bread crumbs, dry Pasta, enriched (white) Rice, white	Whole-grain bread Rolled oats or crushed bran cereal Whole wheat pasta Brown rice, wild rice, bulgur, or pearl barley
FAT	Butter, margarine, shortening, or oil in baked goods	Applesauce or prune puree for half of the butter, shortening, or oil; butter spreads or shortenings specially formulated for baking without trans fats (Note: To avoid dense, soggy, or flat baked goods, don't substitute oil for butter or shortening. Also don't substitute diet, whipped, or tub-style margarine for regular margarine.)
	Butter, margarine, shortening, or oil to prevent sticking	Cooking spray or nonstick pans
	Mayonnaise	Reduced-calorie mayonnaise-type salad dressing or reduced-calorie, reduced-fat mayonnaise
	Oil-based marinades	Wine, balsamic vinegar, fruit juice, or fat-free broth
SUGAR	Sugar	In most baked goods you can reduce the amount of sugar by one-half; intensify sweetness by adding vanilla, nutmeg, or cinnamon.
	Syrup	Pureed fruit, such as applesauce, or low-calorie, sugar-free syrup
	Chocolate chips	Craisins
SAUCES	Soy sauce	Sweet-and-sour sauce, hot mustard sauce, or low-sodium soy sauce
SALT	Salt	Herbs, spices, citrus juices (lemon, lime, orange), rice vinegar, salt-free seasoning mixes or herb blends, low-sodium soy sauce
	Seasoning salts (garlic, celery, or onion salts)	Herb-only seasonings, such as garlic powder, celery seed, or onion flakes, or finely chopped herbs or garlic, celery, or onions

**Watermelon Raspberry
Cleanser, page 59**

CHAPTER 1:

nutrient-rich juices & smoothies

nutrient-rich juices & smoothies

ginger greens

Considered two of the ultimate detox foods, kale and cilantro combine to cleanse your system! Avocado lends a rich, creamy consistency and a healthful dose of good monounsaturated fat.

ingredients

¾ cup baby kale, packed

¼ cup fresh cilantro

¼ ripe avocado, pitted, peeled

1 date, pitted, cut in half

2 kiwis, peeled, cut in quarters

1 teaspoon lime juice

¼-inch piece fresh ginger, peeled

¼ cup coconut water

¼ cup ice

directions

1. Place all of the ingredients into the Small 18-ounce Cup in the order listed.

2. Turn unit ON, then select Auto-iQ™ Nutri Ninja® ULTRA BLEND.

1 SERVING: CALORIES 230; FAT 9G; SODIUM 55MG; POTASSIUM 1250MG; CARBOHYDRATES 37G; SUGAR 13G; FIBER 11G; PROTEIN 7G; VITAMIN A 110%DV; VITAMIN C 330%DV; MAGNESIUM 20%DV; ZINC 6%DV

 NINJA KNOW-HOW FOR AN EXTRA DETOXIFYING BONUS, ADD ½ TEASPOON CHLORELLA POWDER.

ginger pear melon defense

Ginger provides a natural anti-inflammatory and aids in digestion. Choose ripe pears for extra sweetness.

ingredients

1 ripe pear, cored, cut in quarters

½ cup cantaloupe, cut in 1-inch chunks

¼ lemon, peeled, seeded

½-inch piece fresh ginger, peeled

½ cup ice

directions

1. Place all of the ingredients into the Small 18-ounce Cup in the order listed.

2. Turn unit ON, then select Auto-iQ™ Nutri Ninja® ULTRA BLEND.

1 SERVING: CALORIES 130; FAT 0G; SODIUM 15MG; POTASSIUM 440MG; CARBOHYDRATES 35G; SUGAR 23G; FIBER 7G; PROTEIN 1G; VITAMIN A 50%DV; VITAMIN C 70%DV; MAGNESIUM 6%DV; ZINC 2%DV

NINJA KNOW-HOW   ADD 1 TABLESPOON SPANISH BEE POLLEN FOR A SUPER FOOD BOOST

PREP TIME: 5 minutes   SERVINGS: 1   CONTAINER: Small 18-ounce Cup

cool honeydew cleanser

This cool cucumber honeydew refresher is only 80 calories, the perfect stress reducer.

ingredients

¼ medium cucumber,
peeled, cut in half

½ cup honeydew melon,
cut in 1-inch chunks

½ cup fresh pineapple,
1-inch chunks

¼ cup water

¼ cup ice

directions

1. Place all of the ingredients into the Small 18-ounce Cup in the order listed.

2. Turn unit ON, then select Auto-iQ™ Nutri Ninja® BLEND.

1 SERVING: CALORIES 80; FAT 0G; SODIUM 20MG; POTASSIUM 350MG; CARBOHYDRATES 20G; SUGAR 16G; FIBER 2G; PROTEIN 1G; VITAMIN A 2%DV; VITAMIN C 90%DV; MAGNESIUM 6%DV; ZINC 2%DV

 NINJA KNOW-HOW ADD 2 TABLESPOONS TART CHERRY CONCENTRATE FOR A HIGH ANTIOXIDANT SUPER FOOD BOOST.

PREP TIME: 5 minutes   SERVINGS: 1   CONTAINER: Small 18-ounce Cup

antioxidant refresher

The combination of blueberries and red cabbage adds a punch of antioxidant power.

ingredients

⅛ cup chopped red cabbage

½ celery stalk, cut in half

½ green apple, unpeeled, uncored, cut in half

½ cup blueberries

⅓ cup watermelon, 1-inch chunks

½ cup ice

directions

1. Place all of the ingredients into the Small 18-ounce Cup in the order listed.

2. Turn unit ON, then select Auto-iQ™ Nutri Ninja® ULTRA BLEND.

1 SERVING: CALORIES 90; FAT 0G; SODIUM 15MG; POTASSIUM 160MG; CARBOHYDRATES 24G; SUGAR 19G; FIBER 3G; PROTEIN 1G; VITAMIN A 8%DV; VITAMIN C 30%DV; MAGNESIUM 2%DV; ZINC 2%DV

NINJA® KNOW-HOW   ADD 1-2 TABLESPOONS FLAXSEEDS TO ADD THAT EXTRA FIBER TO YOUR DIET.

PREP TIME: 5 minutes   SERVINGS: 1   CONTAINER: Small 18-ounce Cup

spicy pineapple recharge

The many health benefits subscribed to jalapeño pepper are almost endless. Combined with the ginger, pineapple, and orange juice, the bite of the pepper makes this a spicy 130-calorie pick-me-up.

ingredients

¼ **small jalapeño pepper, seeded**

¼-**inch piece fresh ginger, peeled**

½ **lime, peeled, seeded, cut in half**

1 **cup fresh pineapple, 1-inch chunks**

⅓ **cup orange juice**

¼ **cup ice**

directions

1. Place all of the ingredients into the Small 18-ounce Cup in the order listed.

2. Turn unit ON, then select Auto-iQ™ Nutri Ninja® BLEND.

1 SERVING: CALORIES 130; FAT 0G; SODIUM 0MG; POTASSIUM 390MG; CARBOHYDRATES 34G; SUGAR 24G; FIBER 4G; PROTEIN 2G; VITAMIN A 6%DV; VITAMIN C 220%DV; MAGNESIUM 8%DV; ZINC 2%DV

NINJA
KNOW-HOW

RIPE PINEAPPLES WILL IMPART THE PERFECT AMOUNT OF SWEETNESS TO BLEND WITH THE HINT OF HEAT AND FRAGRANT TASTE OF GINGER.

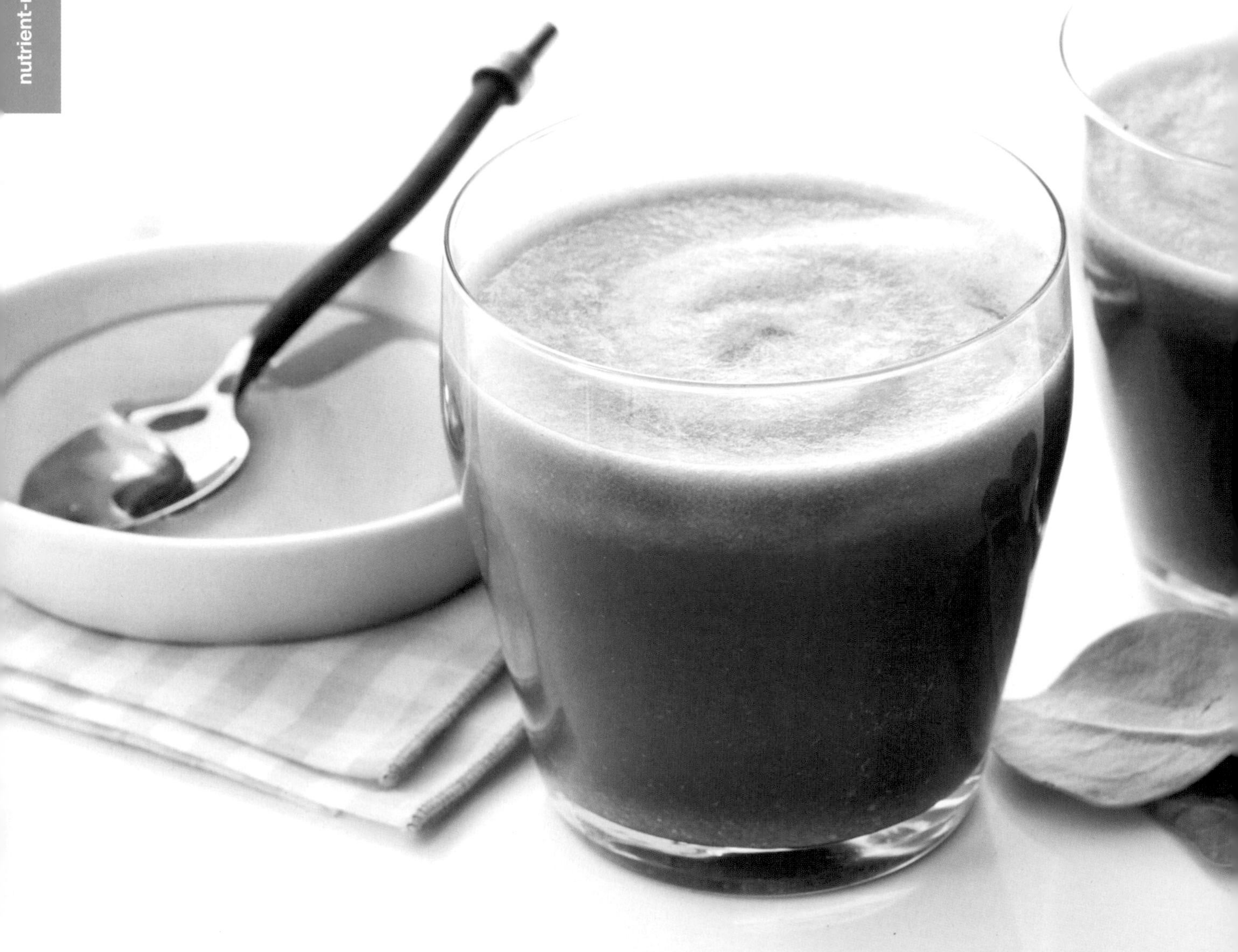

PREP TIME: 5 minutes   SERVINGS: 1   CONTAINER: Small 18-ounce Cup

sweet spinach detox

The combination of citrus with greens will help with the absorption of iron, plus it's a great way to get spinach into your diet!

ingredients

⅓ cup spinach, packed

¼-inch piece fresh ginger, peeled

¾ green apple, unpeeled, uncored, cut in quarters

¼ lemon, peeled, seeded

2 teaspoons agave nectar or honey

⅛ cup apple juice

⅛ cup water

¼ cup ice

directions

1. Place all of the ingredients into the Small 18-ounce Cup in the order listed.

2. Turn unit ON, then select Auto-iQ™ Nutri Ninja® ULTRA BLEND.

1 SERVING: CALORIES 130; FAT 0G; SODIUM 15MG; POTASSIUM 260MG; CARBOHYDRATES 35G; SUGAR 27G; FIBER 4G; PROTEIN 1G; VITAMIN A 20%DV; VITAMIN C 30%DV; MAGNESIUM 4%DV; ZINC 0%DV

NINJA
KNOW-HOW
ADD ½ ORANGE TO ADD TO THE VITAMIN C PUNCH!

PREP TIME: 5 minutes   SERVINGS: 4–6   CONTAINER: 72-ounce Pitcher

avocado-lada

This drink is creamy and delicious; the coconut water gives it a tropical flavor. Plus, it's a great fiber boost.

ingredients

2 ripe avocados, pitted, peeled

2 small bananas

4 cups coconut water

1½ cups frozen pineapple

directions

1. Place all of the ingredients into the Pitcher in the order listed.

2. Turn unit ON, then select Auto-iQ™ FROZEN DRINKS/SMOOTHIES.

1 SERVING: CALORIES 280; FAT 15G; SODIUM 260MG; POTASSIUM 1340MG; CARBOHYDRATES 37G; SUGAR 19G; FIBER 12G; PROTEIN 5G; VITAMIN A 4%DV; VITAMIN C 80%DV; MAGNESIUM 30%DV; ZINC 6%DV

NINJA KNOW-HOW   YOU CAN SUBSTITUTE COCONUT MILK FOR AN EVEN RICHER ENERGY-RICH DRINK.

PREP TIME: 5 minutes   SERVINGS: 4   CONTAINER: 72-ounce Pitcher

south of the border

The boost of cayenne pepper is both a fat burner and helps enhance metabolism.

ingredients

2 ripe avocados, pitted, peeled

¼ cup pineapple

¼ cup fresh cilantro, stems removed

¼ teaspoon cayenne pepper

2 cups water

2 cups frozen mango

directions

1. Place all of the ingredients into the Pitcher in the order listed.

2. Turn unit ON, then select Auto-iQ™ FROZEN DRINKS/SMOOTHIES.

1 SERVING: CALORIES 220; FAT 15G; SODIUM 15MG; POTASSIUM 640MG; CARBOHYDRATES 22G; SUGAR 13G; FIBER 8G; PROTEIN 3G; VITAMIN A 25%DV; VITAMIN C 80%DV; MAGNESIUM 10%DV; ZINC 4%DV

NINJA KNOW-HOW FRESH CILANTRO SHOULD ALWAYS BE STORED IN THE REFRIGERATOR, WITH ROOTS IN A GLASS OF WATER AND LEAVES COVERED WITH A LOOSELY FITTING PLASTIC BAG.

PREP TIME: 5 minutes   SERVINGS: 1   CONTAINER: Small 18-ounce Cup

pear cleanse

Bok choy plus cilantro can help your body's detoxifying process.

ingredients

¾ cup chopped bok choy

¼ cup fresh cilantro

1 ripe pear, cored, cut in quarters

⅛ ripe avocado, pitted, peeled

1 teaspoon lime juice

½ date, pitted

¼ cup holy basil, or tulsi, tea, brewed and chilled

¼ cup ice

directions

1. Place all of the ingredients into the Small 18-ounce Cup in the order listed.

2. Turn unit ON, then select Auto-iQ™ Nutri Ninja® ULTRA BLEND.

1 SERVING: CALORIES 160; FAT 4G; SODIUM 40MG; POTASSIUM 510MG; CARBOHYDRATES 34G; SUGAR 21G; FIBER 8G; PROTEIN 2G; VITAMIN A 50%DV; VITAMIN C 60%DV; MAGNESIUM 8%DV; ZINC 4%DV

 NINJA KNOW-HOW ADD ½ TEASPOON FLAXSEED OIL TO ROUND OUT THE FLAVORS, BRINGING A NUTTY QUALITY WITH ADDED NUTRITION.

PREP TIME: 5 minutes   SERVINGS: 1   CONTAINER: Small 18-ounce Cup

berry healthy

Spinach blends perfectly with the natural sweetness and flavor of the fruit. The kids will not know it's in there.

ingredients

¼ cup spinach, packed

¼ cup water

¼ cup strawberries, hulled

¼ cup blueberries

½ cup fresh mango,
1-inch chunks

¼ cup fresh pineapple,
1-inch chunks

¼ cup ice

directions

1. Place all of the ingredients into the Small 18-ounce Cup in the order listed.

2. Turn unit ON, then select Auto-iQ™ Nutri Ninja® ULTRA BLEND.

1 SERVING: CALORIES 110; FAT 0.5G; SODIUM 10MG; POTASSIUM 310MG; CARBOHYDRATES 26G; SUGAR 21G; FIBER 4G; PROTEIN 2G; VITAMIN A 35%DV; VITAMIN C 130%DV; MAGNESIUM 6%DV; ZINC 2%DV

NINJA KNOW-HOW — ADD 1 TEASPOON FRESH GINGER FOR A SUPER FOOD BOOST.

PREP TIME: 5 minutes   SERVINGS: 1   CONTAINER: Small 18-ounce Cup

broccoli sprout detox

Research has shown that just 2 tablespoons of brocooli sprouts contain as much detoxifying glucoraphanin as 2 pounds of fully mature broccoli.

ingredients

2 tablespoons broccoli sprouts

½ lime, peeled

¼ cup celery with leaves

¼ avocado, pitted, peeled

¼ cup parsley

1 cup water

½ cup frozen raspberries

directions

1. Place all of the ingredients into the Small 18-ounce Cup in the order listed.

2. Turn unit ON, then select Auto-iQ™ Nutri Ninja® ULTRA BLEND.

1 SERVING: CALORIES 128; FAT 7G; SODIUM 44MG; POTASSIUM 490MG; CARBOHYDRATES 16G; SUGAR 4G; FIBER 8G; PROTEIN 2G; VITAMIN A 30%DV; VITAMIN C 80%DV; MAGNESIUM 8%DV; ZINC 4%DV

NINJA KNOW-HOW   YOU CAN USE BROCCOLI SPROUTS AS A SUPER FOOD BOOSTER IN ALMOST ANY SMOOTHIE.

PREP TIME: 5 minutes   SERVINGS: 4   CONTAINER: 72-ounce Pitcher

holiday pear

Tastes like a pear tart with holiday spices and the surprise creaminess of avocado.

ingredients

2 avocados, pitted, peeled

2 pears, cored, cut into chunks

2 tablespoons honey

¾ teaspoon ground cinnamon

¼ teaspoon ground cloves

2½ cups almond milk

1 cup ice

directions

1. Place all of the ingredients into the 72-ounce Pitcher in the order listed.

2. Turn unit ON, then select Auto-iQ™ FROZEN DRINKS/SMOOTHIES.

1 SERVING: CALORIES 270; FAT 17G; SODIUM 120MG; POTASSIUM 720MG; CARBOHYDRATES 32G; SUGAR 17G; FIBER 10G; PROTEIN 3G; VITAMIN A 10%DV; VITAMIN C 25%DV; MAGNESIUM 10%DV; ZINC 6%DV

NINJA KNOW-HOW : MAKE ALMOND MILK IN THE PITCHER. BLEND AT HIGH SPEED UNTIL SMOOTH: 1 CUP ALMONDS (SOAKED OVERNIGHT) AND 2 CUPS WATER. STRAIN, THEN SWEETEN TO TASTE.

PREP TIME: 5 minutes SERVINGS: 4–6 CONTAINER: 72-ounce Pitcher

spiced cucumber

Just like a chilled summer soup, cooling and refreshing, and only 50 calories! The inside temperature of a cucumber can actually be up to 20% cooler than the outside.

ingredients

2 cups chopped English cucumber

1¼ cups cantaloupe, cut in 1-inch chunks

1 jalapeño, seeded

1 cup green seedless grapes

2 cups water

1¼ cups ice

directions

1. Place all of the ingredients into the Pitcher in the order listed.

2. Turn unit ON, then select Auto-iQ™ FROZEN DRINKS/SMOOTHIES.

1 SERVING: CALORIES 50; FAT 0G; SODIUM 15MG; POTASSIUM 290MG; CARBOHYDRATES 13G; SUGAR 10G; FIBER 1G; PROTEIN 1G; VITAMIN A 35%DV; VITAMIN C 40%DV; MAGNESIUM 4%DV; ZINC 2%DV

 NINJA KNOW-HOW USE OTHER TYPES OF CUCUMBERS FOR VARIETY—THEY CAN BE WHITE, YELLOW, AND ORANGE, AND LONG, VERY SHORT, CURVED, STRAIGHT, OVAL, LEMON SHAPED, OR EVEN ROUND.

PREP TIME: 5 minutes   SERVINGS: 1   CONTAINER: Small 18-ounce Cup

super green smoothie

Only 70 calories this tasty green smoothie is the perfect between-meal refresher.

ingredients

¼ cup spinach, packed

1½-inch piece medium cucumber, peeled and cut lengthwise

6 green grapes

½ cup honeydew melon, cut in 1-inch chunks

¼ orange, peeled, cut in half

¼ cup ice

directions

1. Place all of the ingredients into the Small 18-ounce Cup in the order listed.

2. Turn unit ON, then select Auto-iQ™ Nutri Ninja® BLEND.

1 SERVING: CALORIES 70; FAT 0G; SODIUM 25MG; POTASSIUM 420MG; CARBOHYDRATES 18G; SUGAR 15G; FIBER 2G; PROTEIN 1G; VITAMIN A 20%DV; VITAMIN C 60%DV; MAGNESIUM 6%DV; ZINC 2%DV

NINJA
KNOW-HOW

ADD 1 TABLESPOON RAW PARSLEY FOR A SUPER FOOD BOOST.

PREP TIME: 5 minutes   SERVINGS: 1   CONTAINER: Small 18-ounce Cup

lean green ninja

The best-tasting green smoothie you will ever experience! The tropical fruit flavors mask the greens, plus you get a big boost of vitamin C.

ingredients

¼ cup spinach, packed

¼ cup kale leaves, packed

⅓ small banana, peeled

⅓ cup fresh pineapple, 1-inch chunks

⅓ cup fresh mango, 1-inch chunks

⅛ cup water

¼ cup ice

directions

1. Place all of the ingredients into the Small 18-ounce Cup in the order listed.

2. Turn unit ON, then select Auto-iQ™ Nutri Ninja® BLEND.

1 SERVING: CALORIES 100; FAT 0.5G; SODIUM 15MG; POTASSIUM 390MG; CARBOHYDRATES 25G; SUGAR 17G; FIBER 3G; PROTEIN 2G; VITAMIN A 60%DV; VITAMIN C 120%DV; MAGNESIUM 8%DV; ZINC 2%DV

NINJA KNOW-HOW   ADD 1-2 TABLESPOONS FLAX SEEDS FOR AN ADDITIONAL FIBER BOOST.

PREP TIME: 5 minutes   SERVINGS: 4–6   CONTAINER: 72-ounce Pitcher

vitamin c bomb

Big flavors of citrus are paired with cranberry and kiwi for a bright antioxidant wake-me-up, and a great source of Vitamin C.

ingredients

½ grapefruit, peeled, cut in quarters

1 orange, peeled, cut in quarters

2 kiwis, peeled, cut in half

½ cup fresh parsley, stems removed

2 cups cranberry juice

1¼ cups ice

directions

1. Place all of the ingredients into the Pitcher in the order listed.

2. Turn unit ON, then select Auto-iQ™ FROZEN DRINKS/SMOOTHIES.

1 SERVING: CALORIES 120; FAT 0G; SODIUM 10MG; POTASSIUM 270MG; CARBOHYDRATES 29G; SUGAR 23G; FIBER 2G; PROTEIN 1G; VITAMIN A 20%DV; VITAMIN C 210%DV; MAGNESIUM 4%DV; ZINC 2%DV

 NINJA KNOW-HOW | CRANBERRIES FREEZE WELL SO YOU CAN STOCK UP ON THEM DURING THE HOLIDAYS AND USE THEM ALL YEAR LONG.

PREP TIME: 5 minutes   SERVINGS: 1   CONTAINER: Small 18-ounce Cup

veggie power

The vitamin C in the broccoli and tomatoes helps convert the iron in spinach into a form that is more available to the body.

ingredients

¼ cup vine ripe tomato, cut in half

¼ cup spinach

1 celery stalk, cut in quarters

¼ cup broccoli florets

1 tablespoon fresh basil, stems removed

¼ apple, unpeeled, cored

⅛ teaspoon ground black pepper

1 cup water

½ cup ice

directions

1. Place all of the ingredients into the Small 18-ounce Cup in the order listed.

2. Turn unit ON, then select Auto-iQ™ Nutri Ninja® ULTRA BLEND.

1 SERVING: CALORIES 45; FAT 0G; SODIUM 40MG; POTASSIUM 310MG; CARBOHYDRATES 10G; SUGAR 6G; FIBER 3G; PROTEIN 1G; VITAMIN A 35%DV; VITAMIN C 45%DV; MAGNESIUM 6%DV; ZINC 2%DV

NINJA
KNOW-HOW

FOR A DELICIOUS TOPPER TRY SPRINKLING GARLIC POWDER ON TOP.

PREP TIME: 5 minutes   SERVINGS: 1   CONTAINER: Small 18-ounce Cup

mango crush

Mint ramps up the antioxidants. The mango and almond milk give this delicious drink a creamy texture without the cream. Mango is also a great vitamin A boost.

ingredients

¼ cup carrot, peeled

½ lime, peeled

1 teaspoon fresh mint, stems removed

2 teaspoons honey

¾ cup almond milk

¾ cup frozen mango

directions

1. Place all of the ingredients into the Small 18-ounce Cup in the order listed.

2. Turn unit ON, then select Auto-iQ™ Nutri Ninja® BLEND.

1 SERVING: CALORIES 170; FAT 3G; SODIUM 160MG; POTASSIUM 500MG; CARBOHYDRATES 38G; SUGAR 29G; FIBER 5G; PROTEIN 2G; VITAMIN A 140%DV; VITAMIN C 90%DV; MAGNESIUM 8%DV; ZINC 2%DV

NINJA KNOW-HOW

IT IS ESTIMATED THAT THERE ARE OVER 600 VARIETIES OF MINT. MOST ARE EASY TO GROW. TRY GROWING YOUR OWN.

PREP TIME: 5 minutes   SERVINGS: 1   CONTAINER: Small 18-ounce Cup

chocolate almond fusion

Unsweetened cocoa powder is a great ingredient to add indulgence, especially when combined with the flavors of almond and banana.

ingredients

1 small banana

½ cup kale, stems removed

2 teaspoons cocoa powder

1 tablespoon almond butter

1 teaspoon agave nectar

1 cup almond milk

½ cup ice

directions

1. Place all of the ingredients into the Small 18-ounce Cup in the order listed.

2. Turn unit ON, then select Auto-iQ™ Nutri Ninja® BLEND.

1 SERVING: CALORIES 270; FAT 13G; SODIUM 230MG; POTASSIUM 890MG; CARBOHYDRATES 38G; SUGAR 18G; FIBER 7G; PROTEIN 8G; VITAMIN A 80%DV; VITAMIN C 80%DV; MAGNESIUM 30%DV; ZINC 8%DV

NINJA KNOW-HOW   ADD 1 TABLESPOON CACAO POWDER FOR A SUPER FOOD BOOST.

PREP TIME: 5 minutes   SERVINGS: 1   CONTAINER: Small 18-ounce Cup

sunshine pick-me-up

This nutrient extraction is full of fiber and protein and designed as a perfect on-the-go meal replacement.

ingredients

1 small banana, peeled, cut in half

½ medium cucumber, cut in half

1 scoop vanilla protein powder

¾ cup coconut water

½ lime, seeded, peeled

1 cup fresh pineapple, 1-inch chunks

¼ cup ice

directions

1. Place all of the ingredients into the Small 18-ounce Cup in the order listed.

2. Turn unit ON, then select Auto-iQ™ Nutri Ninja® BLEND.

1 SERVING: CALORIES 350; FAT 2.5G; SODIUM 300MG; POTASSIUM 1410MG; CARBOHYDRATES 65G; SUGAR 38G; FIBER 9G; PROTEIN 23G; VITAMIN A 6%DV; VITAMIN C 180%DV; MAGNESIUM 30%DV; ZINC 6%DV

 NINJA KNOW-HOW   ADD 1 TABLESPOON MACA POWDER FOR A SUPER FOOD BOOST.

PREP TIME: 5 minutes   SERVINGS: 6   CONTAINER: 72-ounce Pitcher

my memory booster

Cranberry juice, known for years to support urinary tract health, is used in this drink to add a unique tart flavor.

ingredients

2 lemons, peeled, seeded, cut in half

¼inch piece fresh ginger, peeled

1 pear, cored, cut in quarters

1 cup chopped red cabbage

3 cups cranberry juice

2 cups ice

directions

1. Place all of the ingredients into the Pitcher in the order listed.

2. Turn unit ON, then select Auto-iQ™ FROZEN DRINKS/SMOOTHIES.

1 SERVING: CALORIES 90; FAT 0G; SODIUM 10MG; POTASSIUM 200MG; CARBOHYDRATES 23G; SUGAR 19G; FIBER 2G; PROTEIN 1G; VITAMIN A 4%DV; VITAMIN C 50%DV; MAGNESIUM 4%DV; ZINC 2%DV

NINJA KNOW-HOW | ADD A SPRINKLE OF ORANGE ZEST FOR AN ADDITIONAL SUPER FOOD BOOST.

PREP TIME: 15 minutes   SERVINGS: 4   CONTAINER: 72-ounce Pitcher

autumn balancer

Beat the bloated blues with this slimming sipper.

ingredients

10 ounces steamed sweet potato

2 cups unsweetened almond milk

¼ cup maple syrup

2 teaspoons flaxseed

½ teaspoon ground turmeric

1 teaspoon kosher salt

1½ cups ice

directions

1. Place all of the ingredients into the Pitcher in the order listed.

2. Turn unit ON, then select Auto-iQ™ FROZEN DRINKS/SMOOTHIES.

1 SERVING: CALORIES 130; FAT 2G; SODIUM 590MG; POTASSIUM 310MG; CARBOHYDRATES 28G; SUGAR 17G; FIBER 3G; PROTEIN 2G; VITAMIN A 230%DV; VITAMIN C 15%DV; MAGNESIUM 6%DV; ZINC 2%DV

PREP TIME: 5 minutes   SERVINGS: 1   CONTAINER: Small 18-ounce Cup

cherry café smoothie

A delicious breakfast smoothie to get you started in the morning.

ingredients

1 cup strongly brewed decaf coffee

½ tablespoon agave nectar

1 tablespoon cocoa powder

½ cup nonfat vanilla yogurt

1¼ cups frozen cherries

directions

1. Place all of the ingredients into the Small 18-ounce Cup in the order listed.

2. Turn unit ON, then select Auto-iQ™ Nutri Ninja® ULTRA BLEND.

1 SERVING: CALORIES 225; FAT 1.5G; SODIUM 95MG; POTASSIUM 830MG; CARBOHYDRATES 70G; SUGAR 45G; FIBER 6G; PROTEIN 9G; VITAMIN A 8%DV; VITAMIN C 25%DV; MAGNESIUM 15%DV; ZINC 8%DV

chocolate cherry protein blast

This is a perfect meal replacement shake, packed with 10 grams of fiber and 17 grams of protein.

ingredients

½ ripe avocado, pitted, peeled

1 cup unsweetened almond milk

1 teaspoon unsweetened cocoa powder

1 scoop chocolate protein powder

¾ cup frozen cherries

directions

1. Place all of the ingredients into the Small 18-ounce Cup in the order listed.

2. Turn unit ON, then select Auto-iQ™ Nutri Ninja® ULTRA BLEND.

1 SERVING: CALORIES 470; FAT 18G; SODIUM 220MG; POTASSIUM 950MG; CARBOHYDRATES 64G; SUGAR 36G; FIBER 10G; PROTEIN 17G; VITAMIN A 6%DV; VITAMIN C 20%DV; MAGNESIUM 8%DV; ZINC 4%DV

NINJA KNOW-HOW | TO GIVE THIS A SUPER FOOD VITAMIN C BOOST, ADD 2 TABLESPOONS TART CHERRY JUICE.

PREP TIME: 5 minutes   SERVINGS: 1   CONTAINER: Small 18-ounce Cup

chocolate watercress refresher

A delicious recipe full of micro nutrients from the watercress. Tastes just like chocolate milk.

ingredients

¾ cup watercress

1 small banana, frozen, cut in half

1 cup unsweetened, light coconut milk

2 tablespoons unsweetened cocoa powder

1 tablespoon ground flaxseeds

½ cup ice

directions

1. Place all of the ingredients into the Small 18-ounce Cup in the order listed.

2. Turn unit ON, then select Auto-iQ™ Nutri Ninja® ULTRA BLEND.

1 SERVING: CALORIES 210; FAT 10G; SODIUM 33MG; POTASSIUM 676MG; CARBOHYDRATES 33G; SUGAR 12G; FIBER 8G; PROTEIN 6G; VITAMIN A 30%DV; VITAMIN C 35%DV; MAGNESIUM 40%DV; ZINC 10%DV

NINJA KNOW-HOW

SPRINKLE SOME CINNAMON ON TOP OF THIS DELICIOUS SMOOTHIE FOR A SUPER FOOD BOOST.

PREP TIME: 5 minutes   SERVINGS: 2–4   CONTAINER: 72-ounce Pitcher

watermelon quench

· ·

Wonderfully refreshing source of lycopene, watermelon is loaded with this phytonutrient that boosts heart and bone health.

ingredients

2½ cups watermelon, cut in 1-inch chunks

2 cups pomegranate juice

1 cup frozen peaches

directions

1. Place all of the ingredients into the Pitcher in the order listed.

2. Turn unit ON, then select Auto-iQ™ FROZEN DRINKS/SMOOTHIES.

1 SERVING: CALORIES 220; FAT 1G; SODIUM 25MG; POTASSIUM 900MG; CARBOHYDRATES 55G; SUGAR 50G; FIBER 2G; PROTEIN 2G; VITAMIN A 25%DV; VITAMIN C 35%DV; MAGNESIUM 10%DV; ZINC 4%DV

PREP TIME: 5 minutes   SERVINGS: 1   CONTAINER: Small 18-ounce Cup

pale green jewel up

Adding cabbage kicks up the vitamin C and soluble fiber, which is easy to make part of your regular diet. Only 100 calories per serving.

ingredients

¼ cup chopped green cabbage

½ grapefruit, peeled, cut in half

½ green apple, unpeeled, uncored, cut in half

¼ cup fresh mint

½ cup water

¼ cup ice

directions

1. Place all of the ingredients into the Small 18-ounce Cup in the order listed.

2. Turn unit ON, then select Auto-iQ™ Nutri Ninja® ULTRA BLEND.

1 SERVING: CALORIES 100; FAT 0G; SODIUM 15MG; POTASSIUM 310MG; CARBOHYDRATES 25G; SUGAR 19G; FIBER 5G; PROTEIN 2G; VITAMIN A 30%DV; VITAMIN C 90%DV; MAGNESIUM 6%DV; ZINC 2%DV

PREP TIME: 5 minutes   SERVINGS: 1   CONTAINER: Small 18-ounce Cup

island mood boost

This drink contains 220 calories and 9 grams of fiber, so it is designed to give you a nice prolonged energy release.

ingredients

1 cup coconut water

½ cup pineapple, cut into 1-inch chunks

½ banana

½ cup frozen strawberries

1 teaspoon flaxseed

½ cup frozen mango

directions

1. Place all of the ingredients into the Small 18-ounce Cup in the order listed.

2. Turn unit ON, then select Auto-iQ™ Nutri Ninja® ULTRA BLEND.

1 SERVING: CALORIES 220; FAT 2G; SODIUM 260MG; POTASSIUM 1120MG; CARBOHYDRATES 51G; SUGAR 35G; FIBER 9G; PROTEIN 4G; VITAMIN A 20%DV; VITAMIN C 180%DV; MAGNESIUM 25%DV; ZINC 4%DV

frozen kale cacao

Known as the "queen of greens," kale is recognized for its exceptional nutrient richness, many health benefits, and delicious flavor.

ingredients

¾ cup kale leaves, packed

1 small banana, quartered, frozen

2 dates, pitted halved

1 teaspoon pure cacao powder

1 scoop chocolate protein powder

1¼ cups unsweeteened coconut milk

¼ cup ice

directions

1. Place all of the ingredients into the Regular 24-ounce Cup in the order listed.

2. Turn unit ON, then select Auto-iQ™ Nutri Ninja® ULTRA BLEND.

1 SERVING: CALORIES 346; FAT 8G; SODIUM 96MG; POTASSIUM 830MG; CARBOHYDRATES 50G; SUGAR 29G; FIBER 7G; PROTEIN 26G; VITAMIN A 110%DV; VITAMIN C 120%DV; MAGNESIUM 30%DV; ZINC 10%DV

 NINJA KNOW-HOW ADD 2 TABLESPOONS CACAO NIBS FOR A SUPER FOOD BOOST, WITH THE BENEFITS OF DARK CHOCOLATE WITHOUT SUGAR.

PREP TIME: 5 minutes   SERVINGS: 1   CONTAINER: Small 18-ounce Cup

make mine green

Aloe is a great way to cleanse, and provides a unique sweet flavor to this green drink.

ingredients

½ cup chopped romaine lettuce

¼ cup chopped, seeded green pepper

¼ cup chopped English cucumber

2 tablespoons fresh cilantro, stems removed

¼ lime, peeled

⅛ teaspoon ground black pepper

1 cup aloe vera drink

½ cup ice

directions

1. Place all of the ingredients into the Small 18-ounce Cup in the order listed.

2. Turn unit ON, then select Auto-iQ™ Nutri Ninja® ULTRA BLEND.

1 SERVING: CALORIES 80; FAT 0G; SODIUM 30MG; POTASSIUM 190MG; CARBOHYDRATES 15G; SUGAR 12G; FIBER 2G; PROTEIN 1G; VITAMIN A 50%DV; VITAMIN C 60%DV; MAGNESIUM 4%DV; ZINC 2%DV

NINJA KNOW-HOW

MAKE SURE THAT YOUR ALOE PRODUCT IS PURE GEL, AND NOT A WHOLE LEAF EXTRACT OR JUICE, WHICH CAN CONTAIN CONTROVERSIAL ANTHRAQUINONES SUCH AS ALOIN.

PREP TIME: 5 minutes   SERVINGS: 1   CONTAINER: Small 18-ounce Cup

mental beet booster

Beets are a good source of folates and are a heart-friendly food.

ingredients

3 basil leaves

½ pink grapefruit, peeled, cut in half

½ small beet, peeled, cut in half

1 tablespoon agave nectar

¼ cup water

¼ cup ice

directions

1. Place all of the ingredients into the Small 18-ounce Cup in the order listed.

2. Turn unit ON, then select Auto-iQ™ Nutri Ninja® ULTRA BLEND.

1 SERVING: CALORIES 120; FAT 0G; SODIUM 40MG; POTASSIUM 320MG; CARBOHYDRATES 32G; SUGAR 19G; FIBER 2G; PROTEIN 1G; VITAMIN A 8%DV; VITAMIN C 80%DV; MAGNESIUM 6%DV; ZINC 2%DV

PREP TIME: 5 minutes   SERVINGS: 1   CONTAINER: Small 18-ounce Cup

icy red purifier

Only 94 calories per serving, this is the perfect anytime drink.

ingredients

1 cup watermelon, cut in 1-inch chunks

¾ cup raspberries

¼ cup water

½ cup ice

directions

1. Place all of the ingredients into the Small 18-ounce Cup in the order listed.

2. Turn unit ON, then select Auto-iQ™ Nutri Ninja® BLEND.

1 SERVING: CALORIES 94; FAT 1G; SODIUM 5MG; POTASSIUM 140MG; CARBOHYDRATES 23G; SUGAR 14G; FIBER 7G; PROTEIN 2G; VITAMIN A 10%DV; VITAMIN C 50%DV; MAGNESIUM 6%DV; ZINC 2%DV

PREP TIME: 5 minutes   SERVINGS: 1   CONTAINER: Small 18-ounce Cup

you making me bananas

· ·

Flaxseed milk contains no cholesterol or lactose, making it the perfect substitute for cow's milk. Banana and orange make a delicious combination for this milkshake-like drink.

ingredients

½ orange, peeled, cut in half

¾ cup original flax milk

¼ teaspoon ground nutmeg

1 small banana, frozen, cut in half

directions

1. Place all of the ingredients into the Small 18-ounce Cup in the order listed.

2. Turn unit ON, then select Auto-iQ™ Nutri Ninja® BLEND.

1 SERVING: CALORIES 160; FAT 2.5G; SODIUM 60MG; POTASSIUM 480MG; CARBOHYDRATES 36G; SUGAR 24G; FIBER 4G; PROTEIN 2G; VITAMIN A 10%DV; VITAMIN C 70%DV; MAGNESIUM 8%DV; ZINC 2%DV

 PREP TIME: 5 minutes   SERVINGS: 1   CONTAINER: Small 18-ounce Cup

berries galore

· ·

A fiber and antioxidant-rich "berry delicious" nutrient extraction.

ingredients

½ cup blackberries

¼ cup raspberries

¼ cup blueberries

1 orange, peeled, cut in quarters

¼ cup ice

directions

1. Place all of the ingredients into the Small 18-ounce Cup in the order listed.

2. Turn unit ON, then select Auto-iQ™ Nutri Ninja® ULTRA BLEND.

1 SERVING: CALORIES 130; FAT 1G; SODIUM 0MG; POTASSIUM 430MG; CARBOHYDRATES 31G; SUGAR 21G; FIBER 10G; PROTEIN 3G; VITAMIN A 10%DV; VITAMIN C 160%DV; MAGNESIUM 10%DV; ZINC 4%DV

PREP TIME: 5 minutes   SERVINGS: 1   CONTAINER: Small 18-ounce Cup

shamrock shake smoothie

A truly green smoothie with a great creamy texture from the bananas and almond milk.

ingredients

½ cup unsweetened almond milk

½ cup water

1 tablespoon agave nectar

¼ cup spinach

¼ cup kale, stems removed

¼ cup Swiss chard, stems removed

½ small banana, frozen

½ cup ice

directions

1. Place all of the ingredients into the Small 18-ounce Cup in the order listed.

2. Turn unit ON, then select Auto-iQ™ Nutri Ninja® ULTRA BLEND.

1 SERVING: CALORIES 140; FAT 2G; SODIUM 130MG; POTASSIUM 440MG; CARBOHYDRATES 30G; SUGAR 20G; FIBER 2G; PROTEIN 2G; VITAMIN A 60%DV; VITAMIN C 50%DV; MAGNESIUM 10%DV; ZINC 2%DV

NINJA KNOW-HOW — FREEZE OVERRIPE BANANAS FOR USE IN THIS AND OTHER SMOOTHIES LATER.

PREP TIME: 5 minutes   SERVINGS: 1   CONTAINER: Small 18-ounce Cup

tangerine protein machine

With 20 grams of protein, this delicious drink also has 5 grams of healthy fiber and is loaded with vitamin C and potassium—perfect for breakfast!

ingredients

1 small banana, peeled, cut in half

½ cup spinach, packed

1 scoop vanilla protein powder

1 cup water

1 tangerine, peeled, cut in quarters

½ cup ice

directions

1. Place all of the ingredients into the Small 18-ounce Cup in the order listed.

2. Turn unit ON, then select Auto-iQ™ Nutri Ninja® BLEND.

1 SERVING: CALORIES 270; FAT 2G; SODIUM 70MG; POTASSIUM 780MG; CARBOHYDRATES 45G; SUGAR 26G; FIBER 6G; PROTEIN 20G; VITAMIN A 40%DV; VITAMIN C 60%DV; MAGNESIUM 15%DV; ZINC 2%DV

 NINJA KNOW-HOW — ADD 1 TEASPOON FRESH GINGER FOR A SUPER FOOD BOOST.

PREP TIME: 5 minutes   SERVINGS: 1   CONTAINER: Small 18-ounce Cup

super berry recovery

This is a perfect post-workout drink, naturally fat- and cholesterol-free, and super hydrating.

ingredients

½ cup red seedless grapes

¼ apple, unpeeled, uncored

1 tablespoon vanilla protein powder

½ cup coconut water

¾ cup frozen blueberries

directions

1. Place all of the ingredients into the Small 18-ounce Cup in the order listed.

2. Turn unit ON, then select Auto-iQ™ Nutri Ninja® ULTRA BLEND.

1 SERVING: CALORIES 190; FAT 1.5G; SODIUM 140MG; POTASSIUM 600MG; CARBOHYDRATES 39G; SUGAR 30G; FIBER 6G; PROTEIN 8G; VITAMIN A 2%DV; VITAMIN C 15%DV; MAGNESIUM 10%DV; ZINC 2%DV

 PREP TIME: 5 minutes   SERVINGS: 4–6   CONTAINER: 72-ounce Pitcher

the refueler

A perfect family smoothie to share after a good workout.

ingredients

2 oranges, peeled, cut in quarters

2 small bananas

2 carrots, peeled, chopped

3¼ cups almond milk

2 cups ice

directions

1. Place all of the ingredients into the Pitcher in the order listed.

2. Turn unit ON, then select Auto-iQ™ FROZEN DRINKS/SMOOTHIES.

1 SERVING: CALORIES 130; FAT 3G; SODIUM 190MG; POTASSIUM 660MG; CARBOHYDRATES 27G; SUGAR 15G; FIBER 5G; PROTEIN 3G; VITAMIN A 230%DV; VITAMIN C 70%DV; MAGNESIUM 10%DV; ZINC 2%DV

PREP TIME: 5 minutes   SERVINGS: 1   CONTAINER: Small 18-ounce Cup

mango melon mint fusion

With only 110 calories, this is the perfect vitamin C–packed refresher.

ingredients

½ cup honeydew melon,
cut in 1-inch chunks

½ cup mango, 1-inch chunks

½ cup cantaloupe,
cut in 1-inch chunks

3 mint leaves

½ cup water

¾ cup ice

directions

1. Place all of the ingredients into the Small 18-ounce Cup in the order listed.

2. Turn unit ON, then select Auto-iQ™ Nutri Ninja® BLEND.

1 SERVING: CALORIES 110; FAT 0.5G; SODIUM 35MG; POTASSIUM 540MG; CARBOHYDRATES 26G; SUGAR 24G; FIBER 3G; PROTEIN 2G; VITAMIN A 70%DV; VITAMIN C 120%DV; MAGNESIUM 8%DV; ZINC 2%DV

  PREP TIME: 5 minutes   SERVINGS: 1   CONTAINER: Small 18-ounce Cup

beet & go

A healthy drinkable salad that tastes wonderful. The beets and Swiss chard each help clear toxins from your system.

ingredients

¾ cup cooked beets

¼ cup Swiss chard,
stems removed

¼ inch piece ginger, peeled

¼ apple, uncored, unpeeled

¼ cup chopped carrot,
peeled

1 cup water

½ cup ice

directions

1. Place all of the ingredients into the Small 18-ounce Cup in the order listed.

2. Turn unit ON, then select Auto-iQ™ Nutri Ninja® ULTRA BLEND.

1 SERVING: CALORIES 100; FAT 0G; SODIUM 150MG; POTASSIUM 580MG; CARBOHYDRATES 23G; SUGAR 17G; FIBER 5G; PROTEIN 3G; VITAMIN A 120%DV; VITAMIN C 20%DV; MAGNESIUM 10%DV; ZINC 4%DV

PREP TIME: 5 minutes   SERVINGS: 1   CONTAINER: Small 18-ounce Cup

kale me up

A great, light detox nutrient juice whenever you need a pick-me-up.

ingredients

¼ apple, uncored, unpeeled

½ cup kale, stems removed

¼ cup chopped English cucumber

½ cup seedless green grapes

1 cup water

½ cup ice

directions

1. Place all of the ingredients into the Small 18-ounce Cup in the order listed.

2. Turn unit ON, then select Auto-iQ™ Nutri Ninja® ULTRA BLEND.

1 SERVING: CALORIES 100; FAT 0.5G; SODIUM 25MG; POTASSIUM 400MG; CARBOHYDRATES 24G; SUGAR 17G; FIBER 3G; PROTEIN 2G; VITAMIN A 70%DV; VITAMIN C 80%DV; MAGNESIUM 8%DV; ZINC 2%DV

NINJA
KNOW-HOW

ADD SOME FRESH PINEAPPLE FOR ADDED SWEETNESS.

PREP TIME: 5 minutes   SERVINGS: 1   CONTAINER: Small 18-ounce Cup

can't beet it

A delicious vegetable and fiber-rich, 70 calorie nutrient juice perfect for sustaining energy.

ingredients

½ carrot, peeled, cut in half

½ small beet, peeled, cut in half

1 celery stalk, trimmed, cut in quarters

½ lemon, peeled, seeded

¼-inch piece fresh ginger, peeled

½ orange, peeled, cut in half

¾ cup water

½ cup ice

directions

1. Place all of the ingredients into the Small 18-ounce Cup in the order listed.

2. Turn unit ON, then select Auto-iQ™ Nutri Ninja® ULTRA BLEND.

1 SERVING: CALORIES 70; FAT 0G; SODIUM 75MG; POTASSIUM 440MG; CARBOHYDRATES 18G; SUGAR 11G; FIBER 5G; PROTEIN 2G; VITAMIN A 110%DV; VITAMIN C 90%DV; MAGNESIUM 6%DV; ZINC 2%DV

NINJA KNOW-HOW   ADD ADD 1 TABLESPOON OF SHELLED HEMP SEEDS TO ADD MORE PROTEIN AND MAKE IT A MEAL.

PREP TIME: 5 minutes   SERVINGS: 1   CONTAINER: Small 18-ounce Cup

tropical squeeze smoothie

A delicious tropical yogurt smoothie, perfect as a mid-morning or afternoon pick-me-up.

ingredients

½ small banana

¼ orange, peeled

¼ cup pineapple, cut into 1-inch chunks

1 cup water

½ cup nonfat yogurt

½ cup frozen mango

directions

1. Place all of the ingredients into the Small 18-ounce Cup in the order listed.

2. Turn unit ON, then select Auto-iQ™ Nutri Ninja® BLEND.

1 SERVING: CALORIES 240; FAT 0.5G; SODIUM 100MG; POTASSIUM 620MG; CARBOHYDRATES 53G; SUGAR 44G; FIBER 4G; PROTEIN 8G; VITAMIN A 25%DV; VITAMIN C 120%DV; MAGNESIUM 10%DV; ZINC 6%DV

PREP TIME: 5 minutes   SERVINGS: 1   CONTAINER: Small 18-ounce Cup

a.m. body fuel smoothie

This smoothie is designed to provide sustainable energy. Full of protein, fiber, and energy.

ingredients

1½ cups unsweetened vanilla almond milk

2 tablespoons vanilla organic hemp protein powder

1 tablespoon white chia seeds

½ teaspoon ground Ceylon cinnamon

½ teaspoon orange peel

1 cup frozen blueberries

½ banana, frozen

directions

1. Place all of the ingredients into the Small 18-ounce Cup in the order listed.

2. Turn unit ON, then select Auto-iQ™ Nutri Ninja® ULTRA BLEND.

1 SERVING: CALORIES 347; FAT 12G; SODIUM 277MG; POTASSIUM 991MG; CARBOHYDRATES 46G; SUGAR 20G; FIBER 17G; PROTEIN 19G; VITAMIN A 20%DV; VITAMIN C 15%DV; MAGNESIUM 20%DV; ZINC 4%DV

  PREP TIME: 5 minutes   SERVINGS: 1   CONTAINER: Small 18-ounce Cup

strawberry melon energy blast

Perfect 50-calorie refresher packed with your vitamin C for the day!

ingredients

¼ medium cucumber, peeled, cut in half

4 strawberries, stems removed

¾ cup cantaloupe, cut in 1-inch chunks

¼ cup ice

directions

1. Place all of the ingredients into the Small 18-ounce Cup in the order listed.

2. Turn unit ON, then select Auto-iQ™ Nutri Ninja® BLEND.

1 SERVING: CALORIES 50; FAT 0G; SODIUM 20MG; POTASSIUM 420MG; CARBOHYDRATES 13G; SUGAR 11G; FIBER 2G; PROTEIN 1G; VITAMIN A 80%DV; VITAMIN C 100%DV; MAGNESIUM 6%DV; ZINC 2%DV

PREP TIME: 5 minutes   SERVINGS: 4–6   CONTAINER: 72-ounce Pitcher

autumn harvest

Just like pumpkin pie, but light and nourishing. The flaxseeds and cabbage provide fiber.

ingredients

1½ cups chopped green cabbage

¾ cup pumpkin puree, canned

1 apple, uncored, unpeeled, cut into quarters

¼-inch piece fresh ginger, peeled

¼ cup maple syrup

2 tablespoons flaxseeds

3 cups water

2 cups ice

directions

1. Place all of the ingredients into the Pitcher in the order listed.

2. Turn unit ON, then select Auto-iQ™ FROZEN DRINKS/SMOOTHIES.

1 SERVING: CALORIES 120; FAT 2G; SODIUM 25MG; POTASSIUM 190MG; CARBOHYDRATES 26G; SUGAR 20G; FIBER 5G; PROTEIN 2G; VITAMIN A 120%DV; VITAMIN C 20%DV; MAGNESIUM 8%DV; ZINC 4%DV

NINJA KNOW-HOW
SUBSTITUTE BRUSSELS SPROUTS IN PLACE OF CABBAGE.

PREP TIME: 5 minutes   SERVINGS: 1   CONTAINER: Small 18-ounce Cup

citrus ginger support

Need a vitamin C boost? This delicious refresher contains 190% of your daily vitamin C requirement. Ginger is used not only as food, but also for its aromatic and many health-promoting properties.

ingredients

¼-inch piece fresh ginger, peeled

½ pink grapefruit, peeled, cut in half

½ small orange, peeled, cut in half

½ lime, peeled

½ cup mango, frozen, 1-inch chunks

¼ cup ice

directions

1. Place all of the ingredients into the Small 18-ounce Cup in the order listed.

2. Turn unit ON, then select Auto-iQ™ Nutri Ninja® ULTRA BLEND.

1 SERVING: CALORIES 130; FAT 0.5G; SODIUM 0MG; POTASSIUM 440MG; CARBOHYDRATES 34G; SUGAR 16G; FIBER 5G; PROTEIN 2G; VITAMIN A 25%DV; VITAMIN C 190%DV; MAGNESIUM 6%DV; ZINC 2%DV

 NINJA KNOW-HOW — ADD 2 TEASPOONS ACAI POWDER FOR A SUPER FOOD BOOST.

PREP TIME: 5 minutes   SERVINGS: 1   CONTAINER: Small 18-ounce Cup

3-2-1 immune booster

Kiwi is highly delicious and relatively low on calories. Combined with orange and grapefruit, it makes this a creamy treat to help support the immune system.

ingredients

1 teaspoon dried goji berries

⅓ pink grapefruit, peeled, cut in quarters

1 kiwi, peeled, cut in half

1 orange, peeled, cut in quarters

⅓ cup water

⅓ cup ice

directions

1. Place all of the ingredients into the Small 18-ounce Cup in the order listed.

2. Turn unit ON, then select Auto-iQ™ Nutri Ninja® ULTRA BLEND.

1 SERVING: CALORIES 130; FAT 0.5G; SODIUM 10MG; POTASSIUM 570MG; CARBOHYDRATES 33G; SUGAR 18G; FIBER 6G; PROTEIN 2G; VITAMIN A 10%DV; VITAMIN C 270%DV; MAGNESIUM 8%DV; ZINC 2%DV

PREP TIME: 5 minutes   SERVINGS: 1   CONTAINER: Small 18-ounce Cup

power ball

Blueberries are full of antioxidants and phytonutrients. Start your day off right with this luscious energy booster.

ingredients

1 small banana

¾ cup unsweetened, light coconut milk

½ teaspoon unsweetened cocoa powder

¾ cup frozen blueberries

directions

1. Place all of the ingredients into the Small 18-ounce Cup in the order listed.

2. Turn unit ON, then select Auto-iQ™ Nutri Ninja® ULTRA BLEND.

1 SERVING: CALORIES 190; FAT 5G; SODIUM 15MG; POTASSIUM 440MG; CARBOHYDRATES 38G; SUGAR 22G; FIBER 6G; PROTEIN 3G; VITAMIN A 10%DV; VITAMIN C 20%DV; MAGNESIUM 15%DV; ZINC 4%DV

PREP TIME: 5 minutes   SERVINGS: 4   CONTAINER: 72-ounce Pitcher

cherry oat dream

A great fruit smoothie with the taste of an oatmeal cookie!

ingredients

1 apple, uncored, chopped

2 cups white cranberry juice

1 cup cooked oatmeal, cold

2 cups frozen cherries

directions

1. Place all of the ingredients into the Pitcher in the order listed.

2. Turn unit ON, then select Auto-iQ™ FROZEN DRINKS/SMOOTHIES.

1 SERVING: CALORIES 170; FAT 1G; SODIUM 55MG; POTASSIUM 260MG; CARBOHYDRATES 39G; SUGAR 28G; FIBER 4G; PROTEIN 2G; VITAMIN A 6%DV; VITAMIN C 60%DV; MAGNESIUM 6%DV; ZINC 2%DV

 PREP TIME: 5 minutes   SERVINGS: 1   CONTAINER: Small 18-ounce Cup

strawberry banana smoothie

One of the most popular smoothies ordered in today's smoothie bars. It contains 6 grams of fiber, 8 grams of protein, and 160% of your daily vitamin C requirement.

ingredients

1 small ripe banana, cut in half

¾ cup 1% milk

1 tablespoon agave nectar

1 cup frozen strawberries

directions

1. Place all of the ingredients into the Small 18-ounce Cup in the order listed.

2. Turn unit ON, then select Auto-iQ™ Nutri Ninja® ULTRA BLEND.

1 SERVING: CALORIES 280; FAT 2.5G; SODIUM 85MG; POTASSIUM 870MG; CARBOHYDRATES 60G; SUGAR 43G; FIBER 6G; PROTEIN 8G; VITAMIN A 8%DV; VITAMIN C 160%DV; MAGNESIUM 15%DV; ZINC 8%DV

PREP TIME: 5 minutes   SERVINGS: 1   CONTAINER: Small 18-ounce Cup

citrus spirulina blast

A fresh blast of citrus pumped up with a hint of spirulina rich in vitamins, minerals, and carotenoids.

ingredients

½ grapefruit, peeled, cut in quarters

½ orange, peeled, cut in quarters

¾ cup pineapple, 1-inch chunks

⅛ cup lime juice

1 teaspoon Spirulina

1 cup water

1 cup ice

directions

1. Place all of the ingredients into the Small 18-ounce Cup in the order listed.

2. Turn unit ON, then select Auto-iQ™ Nutri Ninja® ULTRA BLEND.

1 SERVING: CALORIES 150; FAT 0.5G; SODIUM 40MG; POTASSIUM 500MG; CARBOHYDRATES 37G; SUGAR 28G; FIBER 5G; PROTEIN 4G; VITAMIN A 30%DV; VITAMIN C 250%DV; MAGNESIUM 10%DV; ZINC 2%DV

NINJA KNOW-HOW   ADD 2 TABLESPOONS ACAI POWDER FOR A SUPER FOOD BOOST.

PREP TIME: 5 minutes   SERVINGS: 1   CONTAINER: Small 18-ounce Cup

apple almond super juice

. . . .

Almond milk is lactose-free. Almond butter is a great source of vitamin E and contains a nutritional punch. A great protein-filled pick-me-up after a workout or long walk.

ingredients

- 1 Granny Smith apple, peeled, cut in half

- 1 teaspoon almond butter

- 1 scoop protein poweder

- 1 cup unsweetened almond milk

- ½ small banana, peeled, cut in half

- 1 tablespoon white chia seeds

directions

1. Place all of the ingredients into the Small 18-ounce Cup in the order listed.

2. Turn unit ON, then select Auto-iQ™ Nutri Ninja® ULTRA BLEND.

1 SERVING: CALORIES 331; FAT 8G; SODIUM 243MG; POTASSIUM 1020MG; CARBOHYDRATES 43G; SUGAR 27G; FIBER 10G; PROTEIN 22G; VITAMIN A 15%DV; VITAMIN C 30%DV; MAGNESIUM 25%DV; ZINC 4%DV

 NINJA KNOW-HOW AVOCADO CAN BE SUBSTITUTED FOR THE BANANA.

PREP TIME: 5 minutes   SERVINGS: 1   CONTAINER: Small 18-ounce Cup

kick-start my day

A perfect morning starter.

ingredients

¾ cup frozen strawberries

1 tablespoon vanilla protein powder

1 cup orange juice

½ banana

directions

1. Place all of the ingredients into the Small 18-ounce Cup and select IQ-Auto FROZEN DRINKS/SMOOTHIES.

1 SERVING: CALORIES 250; FAT 1G; SODIUM 20MG; POTASSIUM 870MG; CARBOHYDRATES 53G; SUGAR 33G; FIBER 5G; PROTEIN 9G; VITAMIN A 4%DV; VITAMIN C 220%DV; MAGNESIUM 15%DV; ZINC 2%DV

    PREP TIME: 5 minutes   SERVINGS: 6   CONTAINER: 72-ounce Pitcher

sunshine of my life

This drink has citrus with a unique sweet fennel mellow aftertaste.

ingredients

2 oranges, peeled, cut in quarters

1 white grapefruit, peeled, cut in quarters

1 cup chopped fennel

3 cups coconut water

2 cups ice

directions

1. Place all of the ingredients into the Pitcher in the order listed.

2. Turn unit ON, then select Auto-iQ™ FROZEN DRINKS/SMOOTHIES.

1 SERVING: CALORIES 60; FAT 0G; SODIUM 135MG; POTASSIUM 500MG; CARBOHYDRATES 14G; SUGAR 10G; FIBER 3G; PROTEIN 2G; VITAMIN A 2%DV; VITAMIN C 70%DV; MAGNESIUM 10%DV; ZINC 2%DV

 KNOW-HOW IF FENNEL IS UNAVAILABLE, SUBSTITUTE CELERY WITH A ¼ TEASPOON CRUSHED FENNEL OR ANISE OR CARAWAY SEED.

PREP TIME: 5 minutes   SERVINGS: 1   CONTAINER: Small 18-ounce Cup

pear energy

Take on pure pear energy along with the green goodness of spinach.

ingredients

½ pear, cored, chopped

½ cup spinach

½ lemon, peeled

2 teaspoons honey

1 cup green tea

¾ cup ice

directions

1. Place all of the ingredients into the Small 18-ounce Cup in the order listed.

2. Turn unit ON, then select Auto-iQ™ Nutri Ninja® ULTRA BLEND.

1 SERVING: CALORIES 110; FAT 0G; SODIUM 20MG; POTASSIUM 260MG; CARBOHYDRATES 28G; SUGAR 20G; FIBER 4G; PROTEIN 1G; VITAMIN A 30%DV; VITAMIN C 40%DV; MAGNESIUM 6%DV; ZINC 2%DV

PREP TIME: 5 minutes   SERVINGS: 6   CONTAINER: 72-ounce Pitcher

iced orange chocolate blast

Chocolate and orange are a perfect marriage of taste and nutrition.

ingredients

1½ oranges, peeled, cut in quarters

¼ cup cocoa powder

¼ cup agave nectar

1 teaspoon ground cinnamon

2½ cups low-fat milk

1½ cups nonfat vanilla yogurt

¾ cup ice

directions

1. Place all of the ingredients into the Pitcher in the order listed.

2. Turn unit ON, then select Auto-iQ™ FROZEN DRINKS/SMOOTHIES.

1 SERVING: CALORIES 170; FAT 1.5G; SODIUM 90MG; POTASSIUM 370MG; CARBOHYDRATES 32G; SUGAR 27G; FIBER 2G; PROTEIN 7G; VITAMIN A 8%DV; VITAMIN C 30%DV; MAGNESIUM 10%DV; ZINC 8%DV

PREP TIME: 5 minutes   SERVINGS: 1   CONTAINER: Small 18-ounce Cup

peach yogurt smoothie

Peaches, pears, and yogurt pair perfectly with ginger in this smoother loaded with probiotics.

ingredients

⅛-inch piece fresh ginger, peeled

½ pear, cored, cut into chunks

1 tablespoon ground flaxseeds

¾ cup nonfat, plain kefir

¼ cup nonfat yogurt

½ cup frozen peaches

directions

1. Place all of the ingredients into the Small 18-ounce Cup in the order listed.

2. Turn unit ON, then select Auto-iQ™ Nutri Ninja® ULTRA BLEND.

1 SERVING: CALORIES 250; FAT 4G; SODIUM 135MG; POTASSIUM 690MG; CARBOHYDRATES 42G; SUGAR 34G; FIBER 6G; PROTEIN 14G; VITAMIN A 8%DV; VITAMIN C 15%DV; MAGNESIUM 20%DV; ZINC 10%DV

NINJA
KNOW-HOW
ADD AN EXTRA TABLESPOON OF FLAXSEEDS FOR EXTRA FIBER.

Almond Chai Tea, 84

CHAPTER 2:

infused teas & waters

PREP TIME: 5 minutes   **SERVINGS:** 1   **CONTAINER:** Small 18-ounce Cup

two berry tea

. . . .

A calming tea filled with berry-rich antioxidants!

ingredients

½ cup fresh blueberries

1 tablespoon goji berries

½ ripe banana

¾ cup rooibos tea, strongly
brewed, chilled

½ cup ice

directions

1. Place all of the ingredients into the Small 18-ounce Cup in the order listed.

2. Turn unit ON, then select Auto-iQ™ Nutri Ninja® ULTRA BLEND.

1 SERVING: CALORIES 120; FAT 0G; SODIUM 30MG; CARBOHYDRATES 30G; SUGAR 19G; FIBER 4G; PROTEIN 2G

 NINJA **KNOW-HOW** ADD 2 TABLESPOONS TART CHERRY CONCENTRATE FOR A SUPER FOOD BOOST.

PREP TIME: 5 minutes   SERVINGS: 1   CONTAINER: Small 18-ounce Cup

cherry lime rickey-ade

An all-natural energy-ade perfect after a good workout!

ingredients

½ cup frozen cherries

1 tablespoon lime juice

8 ounces coconut water

directions

1. Place all of the ingredients into the Small 18-ounce Cup.

2. Turn unit ON, then select Auto-iQ™ Nutri Ninja® BLEND.

3. Pour mixture through a fine-mesh strainer to extract the flavored water.

1 SERVING: CALORIES 90; FAT 0G; SODIUM 250MG; CARBOHYDRATES 21G; SUGAR 16G; FIBER 4G; PROTEIN 2G

NINJA KNOW-HOW   ADD 1 TABLESPOON CHIA SEEDS FOR YOUR VERY OWN HOMEMADE CHIA FRESCA.

PREP TIME: 5 minutes   SERVINGS: 1   CONTAINER: Small 18-ounce Cup

almond chai tea

Almond chai tea, rich in antioxidants and spices, has been used for thousands of years to promote general health and well-being.

ingredients

3 dates, pitted, cut in half

2 tablespoons raw almonds

¼ ripe banana

1¼ cups chai tea, chilled, strongly brewed

directions

1. Place all of the ingredients into the Small 18-ounce Cup in the order listed.

2. Turn unit ON, then select Auto-iQ™ Nutri Ninja® ULTRA BLEND.

1 SERVING: CALORIES 180; FAT 8G; SODIUM 0MG; CARBOHYDRATES 25G; SUGAR 18G; FIBER 4G; PROTEIN 4G

 PREP TIME: 5 minutes   SERVINGS: 1   CONTAINER: Small 18-ounce Cup

pineapple mint water

Mint is a proven stomach soother and is great for your breath, too.

ingredients

¼ cup fresh pineapple, cut into 1-inch chunks

1 teaspoon fresh mint, stems removed

1½ cups cold water

directions

1. Place all of the ingredients into the Small 18-ounce Cup in the order listed.

2. Turn unit ON, then select Auto-iQ™ Nutri Ninja® BLEND.

1 SERVING: CALORIES 20; FAT 0G; SODIUM 15MG; CARBOHYDRATES 5G; SUGAR 4G; FIBER 1G; PROTEIN 0G

PREP TIME: 5 minutes SERVINGS: 1 CONTAINER: Small 18-ounce Cup

coconut mango energyade

Create your own natural sports drink for active adults and children. High in potassium and perfect for hydration!

ingredients

¼ cup chopped ripe mango

1½ cups coconut water

⅛ cup fresh mint leaves

directions

1. Place all of the ingredients into the Small 18-ounce Cup.

2. Turn unit ON, then select Auto-iQ™ Nutri Ninja® BLEND.

1 SERVING: CALORIES 80; FAT 0G; SODIUM 15MG; CARBOHYDRATES 20G; SUGAR 17G; FIBER 0G; PROTEIN 1G

NINJA KNOW-HOW ADD 2 TABLESPOONS GROUND FLAXSEEDS FOR A SUPER FOOD BOOST.

PREP TIME: 5 minutes SERVINGS: 1 CONTAINER: Small 18-ounce Cup

melon fresca

• •

This a refreshing low-calorie drink, perfect for an afternoon snack.

ingredients

¼ cup cantaloupe, cut in
1-inch chunks

¼ cup watermelon, cut in
1-inch chunks

1½ cups water

⅛ teaspoon sea salt

¼ cup ice

directions

1. Place all of the ingredients into the Small 18-ounce Cup in the order listed.

2. Turn unit ON, then select Auto-iQ™ Nutri Ninja® BLEND.

1 SERVING: CALORIES 25; FAT 0G; SODIUM 320MG; CARBOHYDRATES 7G; SUGAR 6G; FIBER 1G; PROTEIN 0G

NINJA
KNOW-HOW

ADD 2 TEASPOONS ACAI
POWDER FOR A SUPER FOOD
BOOST.

PREP TIME: 5 minutes SERVINGS: 1 CONTAINER: Small 18-ounce Cup

peach hydration

This is a great after-workout refresher.

ingredients

½ lemon, peeled, cut in half

1½ cups coconut water

⅓ cup frozen peaches

directions

1. Place all of the ingredients into the Small 18-ounce Cup in the order listed.

2. Turn unit ON, then select Auto-iQ™ Nutri Ninja® ULTRA BLEND.

1 SERVING: CALORIES 90; FAT 0G; SODIUM 20MG; CARBOHYDRATES 22G; SUGAR 16G; FIBER 1G; PROTEIN 1G

 PREP TIME: 5 minutes SERVINGS: 1 CONTAINER: Small 18-ounce Cup

cherry cooler

Add 2 tablespoons tart cherry concentrate for a super food boost.

ingredients

1½ cups water

½ cup frozen dark sweet cherries

directions

1. Place all of the ingredients into the Small 18-ounce Cup.

2. Turn unit ON, then select Auto-iQ™ Nutri Ninja® ULTRA BLEND.

1 SERVING: CALORIES 45; FAT 0G; SODIUM 15MG; CARBOHYDRATES 11G; SUGAR 9G; FIBER 2G; PROTEIN 1G

Zucchini Quinoa Latkes, 104

CHAPTER 3:

breakfasts

breakfasts

coffee soymoothie

This creamy coffee drink has both almond butter and silken tofu to get you started in the morning!

ingredients

½ cup strongly brewed decaf coffee

⅓ cup silken tofu

2 teaspoons almond butter

⅛ teaspoon cardamom powder

1 tablespoon agave nectar

½ cup ice

directions

1. Place all of the ingredients into the Small 18-ounce Cup in the order listed.

2. Turn unit ON, then select Auto-iQ™ Nutri Ninja® BLEND.

1 SERVING: CALORIES 160; FAT 8G; SODIUM 30MG; CARBOHYDRATES 19G; SUGAR 17G; FIBER 1G; PROTEIN 6G

 NINJA KNOW-HOW   ADD 1 TABLESPOON CACAO POWDER FOR A SUPER FOOD BOOST.

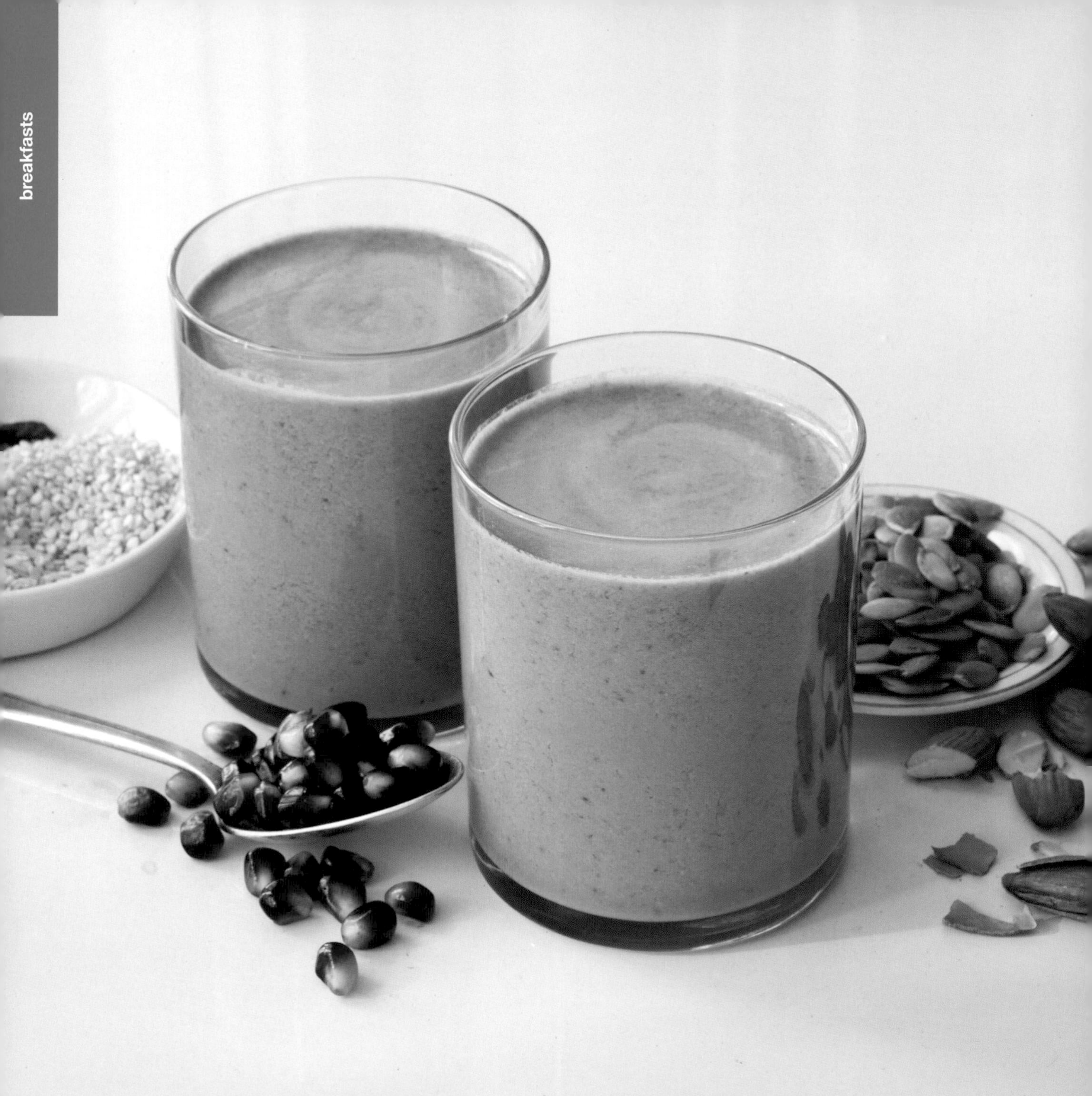

PREP TIME: 7 minutes   SERVINGS: 1   CONTAINER: Small 18-ounce Cup

trail mix in a glass

Great for those with an active lifestyle. All the flavors of a trail mix whipped up in a nourishing breakfast.

ingredients

2 tablespoons raw unsalted almonds

2 tablespoons raw unsalted pumpkin seeds

2 teaspoons raw sesame seeds

2 tablespoons goji berries

2 tablespoons pomegranate juice

¾ cup unsweetened vanilla almond milk

2 tablespoons honey

½ cup ice

directions

1. Place all of the ingredients into the Small 18-ounce Cup in the order listed.

2. Turn unit ON, then select Auto-iQ™ Nutri Ninja® ULTRA BLEND.

1 SERVING: CALORIES 480; FAT 23G; SODIUM 210MG; CARBOHYDRATES 57G; SUGAR 45G; FIBER 5G; PROTEIN 13G

 NINJA KNOW-HOW

ADD 1 TABLESPOON SPANISH BEE POLLEN FOR A SUPER FOOD BOOST.

PREP TIME: 5 minutes   SERVINGS: 1   CONTAINER: Small 18-ounce Cup

banana & oats

•••

You will love this portable oatmeal breakfast loaded with micronutrient-rich walnuts and fruit.

ingredients

1 small banana

1 tablespoon walnuts

1 cup fat-free milk

½ cup cooked oatmeal, cold

¼ teaspoon ground cinnamon

½ cup nonfat vanilla yogurt

directions

1. Place all of the ingredients into the Small 18-ounce Cup in the order listed.

2. Turn unit ON, then select Auto-iQ™ Nutri Ninja® BLEND.

1 SERVING: CALORIES 410; FAT 7G; SODIUM 180MG; CARBOHYDRATES 74G; SUGAR 45G; FIBER 5G; PROTEIN 18G

NINJA KNOW-HOW | TO MAKE SURE YOUR YOGURT CONTAINS ACTIVE CULTURES, CHECK THE LABEL.

PREP TIME: 10 minutes   COOK TIME: 3 minutes   SERVINGS: 2   CONTAINER: Jumbo Multi-Serve 32-ounce Cup

tomato basil scramble

This recipe is an easy and simple way to make fluffy eggs and veggies in the morning!

ingredients

4 large eggs

¼ cup vine-ripe tomato, deseeded

¼ cup mozzarella

¼ cup fresh basil, loosely packed

⅛ teaspoon kosher salt

⅛ teaspoon ground black pepper

2 teaspoons unsalted butter

directions

1. Place the eggs, tomato, mozzarella, basil, salt, and black pepper into the Jumbo Multi-Serve 32-ounce Cup. Turn unit ON. Hold down Auto-iQ™ PULSE until finely chopped.

2. In a nonstick sauté pan, heat the butter over medium-high heat. Add the egg mixture, then cook, stirring frequently until fluffy and cooked through.

3. Divide into two servings after cooking.

1 SERVING: CALORIES 220; FAT 16G; SODIUM 350MG; CARBOHYDRATES 2G; SUGAR 1G; FIBER 0G; PROTEIN 17G

 NINJA KNOW-HOW YOU CAN SUBSTITUTE 6 LARGE EGG WHITES FOR A LOWER-CHOLESTEROL BREAKFAST.

PREP TIME: 5 minutes + 1 hour rest   COOK TIME: 5 minutes   SERVINGS: 4   CONTAINER: 72-ounce Pitcher

buckwheat boost pancakes

Wholesome low-fat pancakes are great on their own or topped with some fresh fruit.

ingredients

½ cup buckwheat groats

½ cup all-purpose flour

1¼ teaspoons baking powder

1 teaspoon sugar

½ teaspoon salt

1 egg

3 tablespoons vegetable oil

2 tablespoons honey

¾ cup skim milk

directions

1. Place the buckwheat groats into the Pitcher, turn unit ON, and select HIGH. Blend for 15 seconds or until groats are ground into a fine flour.

2. Add the all-purpose flour, baking powder, sugar, salt, egg, oil, honey, and milk to the Pitcher and select MEDIUM. Blend until smooth. Let batter set for 1 hour.

3. On a lightly oiled griddle or sauté pan over medium heat, pour pancake batter in desired size and cook until small bubbles form. Flip and continue cooking until center is puffed and springs back when gently pushed.

1 SERVING: CALORIES 290; FAT 12G; SODIUM 470MG; CARBOHYDRATES 40G; SUGAR 11G; FIBER 3G; PROTEIN 7G

 NINJA KNOW-HOW ┊ FOR AN EVEN HEALTHIER VERSION SUBSTITUTE WHOLE WHEAT FLOUR FOR THE ALL-PURPOSE FLOUR.

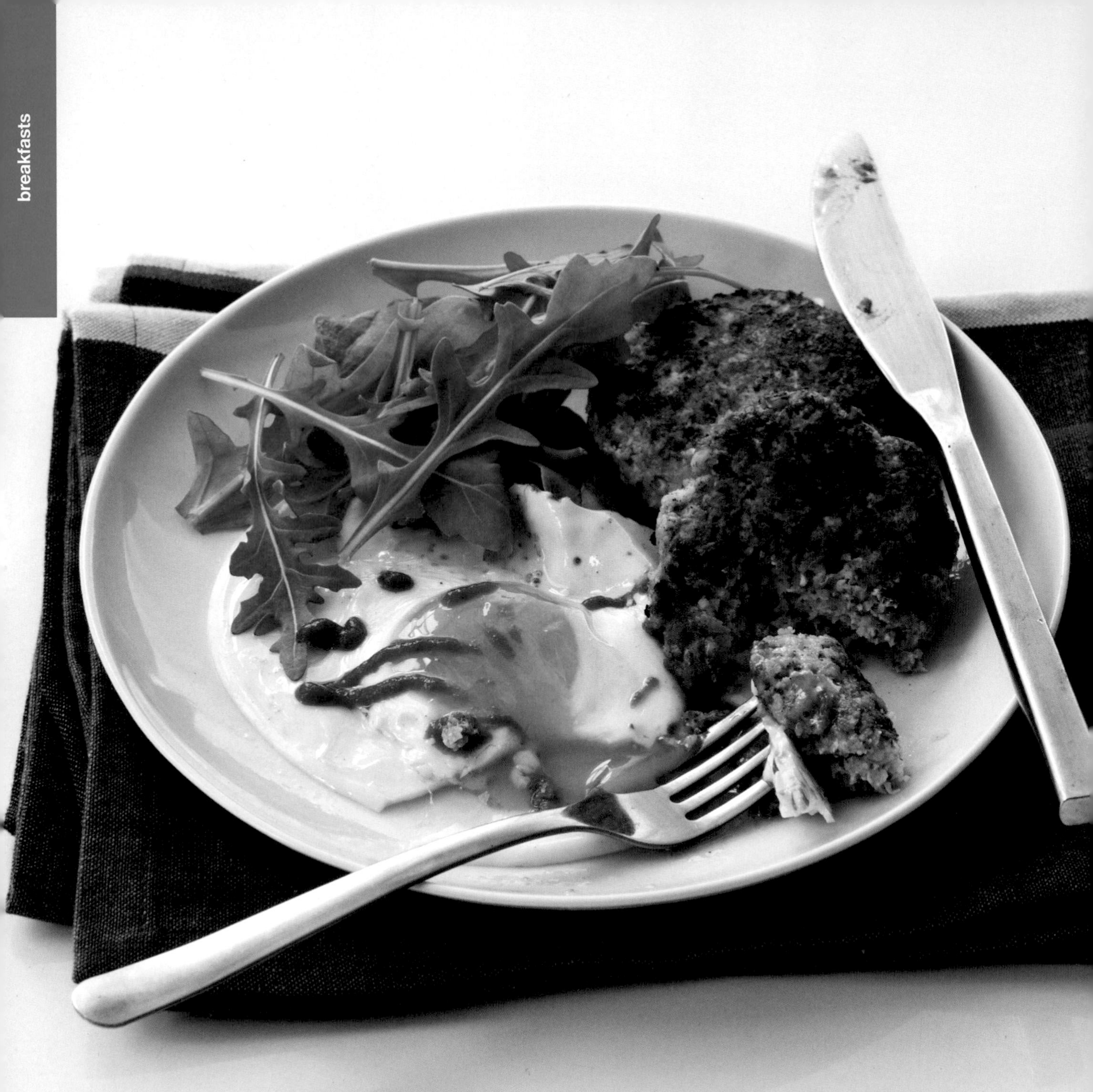

chicken apple sausage

Once you start making your own homemade sausage in your Ninja, you will want to try more.

ingredients

1 tablespoon olive oil

1 small onion, peeled, cut in quarters

2 apples, peeled, cored, cut in quarters

⅓ cup fresh sage leaves

1 pound boneless skinless chicken thighs (or breast if you prefer white meat), 2-inch chunks

Pinch of cinnamon

¾ teaspoon fresh ground pepper

¾ teaspoon kosher salt

directions

1. Place the onion, apples, and sage in the Food Processor Bowl. Turn unit ON, then hold down Auto-iQ™ PULSE until finely chopped.

2. Heat the olive oil in a medium skillet. Add the onion and apples, sautéeing several minutes, until soft. Remove from heat and place in a large bowl.

3. Place chicken thighs into the Food Processor Bowl. Hold down Auto-iQ™ PULSE until finely ground. Add the ground chicken to the bowl with the onion and apple mix. Add the cinnamon and season with salt and pepper. Mix well, using your hands.

4. Preheat oven to 350°F. Form mixture into eight patties and bake on a parchment-lined cookie sheet for 10–12 minutes, or until fully cooked.

1 SERVING: CALORIES 100; FAT 4G; SODIUM 230MG; CARBOHYDRATES 5G; SUGAR 4G; FIBER 1G; PROTEIN 11G

NINJA KNOW-HOW: YOU CAN SUBSTITUTE TURKEY FOR THE CHICKEN.

PREP TIME: 15 minutes + 4 hours rest COOK TIME: 25 minutes SERVINGS: 8 CONTAINER: 56-Ounce Food Processor Bowl

spinach & feta egg strata

This recipe is wonderfully delicious. Great for a morning family brunch.

ingredients

5 large eggs

1 cup half-and-half

½ cup Monterey Jack cheese, cubed

½ cup feta cheese, cubed

¼ teaspoon ground nutmeg

½ teaspoon salt

¼ teaspoon black pepper

1 cup cooked spinach, well drained (about 6 cups fresh)

Cooking spray

1 loaf day-old French bread, crusts removed, torn into bite-sized pieces

directions

1. Preheat oven to 350°F. Add the eggs, half-and-half, Monterey Jack cheese, feta cheese, nutmeg, salt, and pepper to the Food Processor Bowl.

2. Turn unit ON, then hold down Auto-iQ™ PULSE for 5 pulses. Remove the lid and add the well-drained spinach. Hold down Auto-iQ™ PULSE for 2 additional pulses.

3. Coat a round 9-inch baking pan with cooking spray. Place the bread into the pan and pour the spinach and egg mixture over the bread. Place into the fridge for 4 hours to allow the egg mixture to soak into the bread.

4. Place the pan onto the middle rack in the oven and bake for 25 minutes. Serve hot.

1 SERVING: CALORIES 310; FAT 12G; SODIUM 660MG; CARBOHYDRATES 35G; SUGAR 2G; FIBER 2G; PROTEIN 16G

NINJA KNOW-HOW: YOU CAN SUBSTITUTE ANY DAY-OLD BREAD.

PREP TIME: 5 minutes   SERVINGS: 1   CONTAINER: Small 18-ounce Cup

top o' the morning

A perfect on-the-go breakfast filled with protein, potassium, and vitamin C.

ingredients

1 small banana, peeled, cut in quarters

½ teaspoon ground cinnamon

1 cup unsweetened almond milk

1 orange, peeled, cut in quarters

½ cup ice

directions

1. Place all of the ingredients into the Small 18-ounce Cup in the order listed.

2. Turn unit ON, then select Auto-iQ™ Nutri Ninja® ULTRA BLEND.

1 SERVING: CALORIES 327; FAT 7G; SODIUM 223MG; CARBOHYDRATES 50G; SUGAR 25G; FIBER 10G; PROTEIN 21G

 **NINJA KNOW-HOW** ADD 2 TEASPOONS GROUND FLAXSEED FOR A SUPER FOOD BOOST.

PREP TIME: 20 minutes   COOK TIME: 10 minutes   SERVINGS: 4   CONTAINER: 56-ounce Food Processor Bowl

zucchini quinoa latkes

A lighter delicious twist to traditional potato pancakes with added protein from the quinoa.

ingredients

2 medium zucchini, cut in thirds

2 large eggs

½ teaspoon kosher salt

½ teaspoon ground black pepper

¼ cup matzo meal

½ cup quinoa, cooked

Olive oil for sautéing

½ cup sour cream

2 tablespoons chives

directions

1. Place the zucchini, eggs, salt, and black pepper into the Food Processor Bowl. Turn unit ON. Hold down Auto-iQ™ PULSE until finely chopped.

2. Place mixture into a mixing bowl, then add the matzo meal and cooked quinoa, stirring to combine.

3. In a nonstick sauté pan, heat the olive oil over medium heat. Drop a spoonful of the batter into the oil and press lightly to flatten. Cook for 2 minutes per side or until golden brown.

4. To serve, top each latke with sour cream and chives.

1 SERVING: CALORIES 220; FAT 15G; SODIUM 290MG; CARBOHYDRATES 15G; SUGAR 3G; FIBER 2G; PROTEIN 7G

NINJA
KNOW-HOW
SERVE WITH LIGHT OR FAT-FREE SOUR CREAM OR APPLE SAUCE.

PREP TIME: 15 minutes + 4 hours rest   COOK TIME: 45 minutes   REST TIME: 30 minutes   SERVINGS: 6–8   CONTAINER: 56-ounce Food Processor

breakfasts

chorizo & pepper strata

This is a high-energy breakfast with a little bit of wake-me-up kick.

ingredients

6 large eggs

2 cups low-fat milk

¼ teaspoon kosher salt

¼ teaspoon ground black pepper

1 tablespoon vegetable oil

½ pound chorizo, chopped

1 poblano pepper, seeded, chopped

½ medium onion, chopped

½ pound whole wheat bread, cut into ½-inch strips

1 cup shredded sharp Cheddar cheese

2 tablespoons chopped fresh cilantro

1 avocado, pitted, sliced

directions

1. Preheat oven to 350°F.

2. Lightly coat a 9 x 9 baking dish with cooking spray.

3. Place the eggs, milk, salt, and black pepper into the Food Processor Bowl. Turn unit ON and select MEDIUM. Blend until smooth.

4. Heat oil in a sauté pan, add chorizo, and sauté on medium heat until browned, about 4 minutes.

5. Add the pepper and onion and cook for 6 minutes.

6. Arrange half the bread slices in the prepared baking dish. Pour half of the egg mixture on top. Add half the chorizo and pepper mixture, spread evenly, then top with cheese, pressing to submerge ingredients. Repeat layering the bread, egg, and chorizo mixture, and cheese.

7. Let strata stand for 30 minutes at room temperature before baking. Bake uncovered for 40 minutes or until a knife inserted into the center comes out clean. Remove from oven and let stand for 5 minutes, then top with cilantro and avocado.

1 SERVING: CALORIES 540; FAT 35G; SODIUM 890MG; CARBOHYDRATES 30G; SUGAR 8G; FIBER 6G; PROTEIN 29G

NINJA KNOW-HOW | SUBSTITUTE LOW-FAT CHEDDAR CHEESE AND CHICKEN APPLE SAUSAGE FOR A LOWER-FAT RECIPE.

PREP TIME: 15 minutes   COOK TIME: 18–20 minutes   SERVINGS: 4   CONTAINER: 56-ounce Food Processor Bowl

turkey hash

A wonderfully delicious, unique, healthier variation of hash.

ingredients

½ medium onion, cut into
1-inch chunks

½ red bell pepper, cut into
1-inch chunks

1 clove garlic

1 pound turkey breast, cut in
1-inch chunks

1 tablespoon vegetable oil

1 pound sweet potato,
peeled, chopped, cooked

¾ cup low-sodium chicken
broth

1 teaspoon dried thyme

¾ teaspoon kosher salt

½ teaspoon ground black
pepper

¼ cup chopped green onion

directions

1. Place the onion, red pepper, garlic, and turkey into the Food Processor Bowl. Turn unit ON, then hold down Auto-iQ™ PULSE until finely chopped.

2. Heat oil in a stockpot, add mixture, and sauté on medium heat for 8 minutes.

3. Add the cooked sweet potatoes, chicken broth, thyme, salt, black pepper, and green onion and cook for 10 minutes or until turkey is cooked through, stirring occasionally.

1 SERVING: CALORIES 250; FAT 4G; SODIUM 1690MG; CARBOHYDRATES 31G; SUGAR 10G; FIBER 5G; PROTEIN 25G

NINJA KNOW-HOW   SERVE WITH SCRAMBLED EGG WHITES FOR A COMPLETE BREAKFAST.

PREP TIME: 10 minutes   COOK TIME: 15 minutes   SERVINGS: 2   CONTAINER: 56-ounce Food Processor Bowl

spicy sausage burrito

This is just spicy enough to give it a south-of-the-border zing.

ingredients

½ medium onion

½ green bell pepper, seeded

1 teaspoon chipotle in adobo sauce

¾ cup crushed tomato

1 clove garlic

1 tablespoon chili powder

2 teaspoons cumin

1 teaspoon dried oregano

½ cup low-sodium chicken broth

¼ teaspoon kosher salt

2 7-inch whole wheat flour tortillas, warmed

1½ cups cooked turkey breakfast sausage

4 large eggs, scrambled

½ cup low-fat Colby Jack cheese

directions

1. Place the onion, green pepper, chipotle into the Food Processor Bowl. Turn unit ON and hold down Auto-iQ™ PULSE until desired chop.

2. Place the onion, green pepper, chipotle, crushed tomato, garlic, chili powder, cumin, oregano, chicken broth, and salt into the Food Processor Bowl. Turn unit ON. Select MEDIUM and blend until smooth. Place mixture in a saucepot, bring to a boil, then reduce to a simmer for 10 minutes.

3. Lay the tortilla on the work surface and top with turkey sausage, scrambled eggs, and cheese. Roll to close.

4. To serve, place burrito on plate and top with warm sauce.

1 SERVING: CALORIES 500; FAT 20G; SODIUM 1660MG; CARBOHYDRATES 42G; SUGAR 12G; FIBER 8G; PROTEIN 40G

NINJA KNOW-HOW   YOU CAN SUBSTITUTE CHICKEN SAUSAGE FOR THE TURKEY.

PREP TIME: 15 minutes   COOK TIME: 35 minutes   REST TIME: 30 minutes   SERVINGS: 6–8   CONTAINER: 56-ounce Food Processor Bowl

monte cristo casserole

If you love a Monte Cristo sandwich, you will love this casserole.

ingredients

8 ounces low-sodium deli turkey

8 ounces 98% fat-free deli ham

8 ounces Swiss cheese, chunked

6 large eggs

2 cups low-fat milk

½ loaf French bread, chopped

¾ cup low-sugar strawberry preserves

directions

1. Preheat oven to 350°F.

2. Lightly coat a loaf pan with cooking spray.

3. Place the turkey, ham, and cheese into the Food Processor Bowl. Turn unit ON. Hold down Auto-iQ™ PULSE until finely chopped. Remove ingredients and set aside.

4. Place the eggs and milk into the Food Processor Bowl. Turn unit ON. Select MEDIUM and blend until smooth.

5. Place the egg mixture into a mixing bowl and add the bread. Stir to coat and let sit for 30 minutes to absorb the egg mixture.

6. Arrange half the bread mixture in the prepared baking dish. Top with the turkey mixture and dollop the preserves throughout. Place remaining bread mixture on top, pressing to submerge ingredients.

7. Bake uncovered for 35 minutes or until a knife inserted into the center comes out clean.

1 SERVING: CALORIES 380; FAT 12G; SODIUM 720MG; CARBOHYDRATES 39G; SUGAR 16G; FIBER 1G; PROTEIN 26G

NINJA KNOW-HOW : SUBSTITUTE WHOLE GRAIN BREAD FOR FRENCH BREAD FOR ADDED FIBER.

PREP TIME: 5 minutes   SERVINGS: 1   CONTAINER: Small 18-ounce Cup

orange you thirsty

A perfect go-to breakfast alternative.

ingredients

¼ cup cantaloupe, cut in 1-inch chunks

¼ cup lychee, canned, drained

½ orange, peeled

½ cup water

⅛ teaspoon cardamom powder

½ cup nonfat Greek yogurt

directions

1. Place all of the ingredients into the Small 18-ounce Cup in the order listed.

2. Turn unit ON, then select Auto-iQ™ Nutri Ninja® BLEND.

1 SERVING: CALORIES 130; FAT 0G; SODIUM 80MG; CARBOHYDRATES 28G; SUGAR 23G; FIBER 3G; PROTEIN 6G

 NINJA® KNOW-HOW | IF UNAVAILABLE, YOU CAN ALSO ORDER FRESH LYCHEES OR LYCHEE PUREE ONLINE.

Chicken Pot Pie, 137

CHAPTER 4:

soups, sauces & entrées

PREP TIME: 25 minutes   COOK TIME: 20 minutes   SERVINGS: 2 cups   CONTAINER: 56-ounce Food Processor

kale & sunflower pesto

A new twist on an old favorite! A great way to use up those extra greens—spinach works well, too!

ingredients

½ **medium bunch kale, stems removed**

¼ **cup fresh basil, packed**

1 **large clove garlic**

¼ **cup unsalted roasted sunflower seeds**

2 **tablespoons Parmesan cheese**

½ **lemon, zest and juice**

Sea salt to taste

Freshly ground pepper

¼ **cup olive oil plus more as needed**

directions

1. Bring 4 quarts of salted water to a boil. Blanch the kale leaves for 30 seconds and upon removal, immediately plunge into ice water. Squeeze the kale leaves dry and set aside.

2. Add the kale, basil, garlic, sunflower seeds, Parmesan, lemon juice/zest, olive oil, and a pinch of salt and pepper to the Food Processor Bowl.

3. Turn unit ON, then hold down Auto-iQ™ PULSE for 5 pulses. Select MEDIUM and blend until desired pesto consistency is achieved. Add more oil if needed. Enjoy atop your favorite pasta or as a delicious dip for your next dinner party!

1 SERVING: CALORIES 45; FAT 4G; SODIUM 15MG; CARBOHYDRATES 2G; SUGAR 0G; FIBER 0G; PROTEIN 1G

 NINJA KNOW-HOW | ROAST YOUR OWN RAW SUNFLOWER SEEDS. SPREAD A THIN LAYER OF SEEDS IN A SKILLET, SET TO MEDIUM-HIGH, AND TOSS UNTIL THEY TURN A LIGHT BROWN.

pineapple cilantro dipping sauce

Of all the bright green herbs out there, cilantro—the fresh, leafy stalks of the coriander plant—are loved by the millions who pile it on soups, salsas, wraps, and roll-ups.

ingredients

3 cups fresh pineapple, cut in 1-inch chunks

1½ small serrano chiles, seeded

1 small white onion, peeled, cut in quarters

½ cup fresh cilantro

4 tablespoons freshly squeezed lime juice

3 tablespoons coconut oil

Salt and pepper to taste

directions

1. Place all of the ingredients into the Pitcher.

2. Turn unit ON and select LOW. Blend for 15 seconds.

1 SERVING: CALORIES 20; FAT 1.5G; SODIUM 0MG; CARBOHYDRATES 2G; SUGAR 2G; FIBER 0G; PROTEIN 0G

NINJA KNOW-HOW: WRAP CILANTRO IN A WET PAPER TOWEL AND STORE IN THE CRISPER DRAWER TO KEEP FRESH AND CRISP.

PREP TIME: 10 minutes **SERVINGS:** 10–12 **CONTAINER:** Small 18-ounce Cup

passion fruit mustard dressing

Try this dressing served over greens, fruit, or even a chicken breast.

ingredients

½ cup frozen passion fruit
pulp, thawed

2 tablespoons Dijon mustard

¼ cup rice wine vinegar

3 tablespoons honey

2 tablespoons fresh thyme,
stems removed

½ teaspoon kosher salt

3 tablespoons extra-virgin
olive oil

¾ cup fat-free sour cream

directions

1. Place all of the ingredients into the Small 18-ounce Cup in the order listed.

2. Turn unit ON, select LOW, then blend for 15 seconds.

1 SERVING: CALORIES 30; FAT 1.5G; SODIUM 55MG; CARBOHYDRATES 4G; SUGAR 3G; FIBER 0G; PROTEIN 0G

NINJA KNOW-HOW

YOU CAN SUBSTITUTE GRADE B MAPLE SYRUP FOR THE HONEY.

fresh & healthy ketchup relish

It's easy to make your own homemade ketchup relish for only 5 calories a serving with the Ninja.

ingredients

¾ cup yellow onion, peeled, cut in quarters, divided

½ red bell pepper, seeded, chopped

1 clove garlic

2 vine-ripe tomatoes, seeded, cut in quarters

1 tablespoon plus 2 teaspoons apple cider vinegar

½ teaspoon molasses

¼ teaspoon ground black pepper

¾ cup kosher baby dill pickles, cut in half

1 tablespoon Dijon mustard

directions

1. Place ½ cup onion, red bell pepper, garlic, tomato, vinegar, molasses, and ground black pepper into the Small 18-ounce Cup. Turn unit ON and hold down Auto-iQ™ PULSE. Blend until smooth.

2. Pour the tomato mixture into a 2-quart saucepot and cook at medium-low heat for 25 minutes, stirring occasionally.

3. Remove from the heat and pour into an airtight container and refrigerate for 1 hour.

4. Place the remaining ¼ cup onion, pickles, Dijon mustard, and the cooled tomato mixture into the Small 18-ounce Cup. Turn unit ON and hold down Auto-iQ™ PULSE until desired chop.

1 SERVING: CALORIES 5; FAT 0G; SODIUM 40MG; CARBOHYDRATES 1G; SUGAR 1G; FIBER 0G; PROTEIN 0G

 NINJA KNOW-HOW IN A COVERED CONTAINER, CHILL THE RELISH OVERNIGHT IN THE REFRIGERATOR TO HELP DEVELOP AND MARRY THE FLAVORS.

PREP TIME: 15 minutes **COOK TIME:** 15 minutes **SERVINGS:** 2 cups **CONTAINER:** Small 18-ounce Cup

tandoori marinade

This delicious tandoori marinade, perfect for lamb, is also a great complement to grilled meats and seafood.

ingredients

2 ounces dried ancho chili peppers

1 teaspoon fresh ginger

2 cloves garlic, peeled

½ cup fresh cilantro, stems removed

2 tablespoons garam masala powder

⅛ teaspoon ground nutmeg

1 tablespoon freshly squeezed lemon juice

1 cup nonfat Greek yogurt

½ cup cold water

directions

1. Place the dried ancho chili peppers into a small saucepot and pour just enough water to cover the peppers. Bring to a boil, reduce to a simmer, and cook for 10 minutes. Strain peppers and then cool.

2. Remove the top and seeds from the peppers.

3. Place all of the ingredients into the Small 18-ounce Cup in the order listed. Turn unit ON, then select Auto-iQ™ Nutri Ninja® BLEND.

1 SERVING: CALORIES 35; FAT 0.5G; SODIUM 15MG; CARBOHYDRATES 5G; SUGAR 1G; FIBER 1G; PROTEIN 3G

NINJA KNOW-HOW — COOK THE SPICES FOR ADDED FLAVOR OR SIMPLY MIX AND USE.

PREP TIME: 30 minutes **COOK TIME:** 30 minutes **SERVINGS:** 2–4 **CONTAINER:** 72-ounce Pitcher

sun-dried tomato sauce

It is so easy to make your own fresh homemade sauce, filled with lycopene. You also control the sugar, not what is found in store-bought sauces.

ingredients

1 onion, peeled, cut in quarters

1 tablespoon canola oil

4 cloves garlic, peeled

1 can (28 ounces) whole tomatoes and juice

6 ounces sun-dried tomatoes packed in olive oil

½ cup dry red wine

½ teaspoon red pepper flakes

¼ bunch basil, chopped
2 tablespoons reserved for garnish

Salt and pepper to taste

directions

1. Place the onion and the garlic into the Pitcher. Turn unit ON, then hold down Auto-iQ™ PULSE until roughly chopped.

2. Heat the oil in a medium saucepan over medium heat and sauté the onions and garlic for 5 minutes, until softened.

3. Add the tomatoes with juice, sun-dried tomatoes, red wine, and red pepper flakes to the Pitcher. Select LOW and blend for 15 seconds, until a chunky consistency is achieved.

4. Add the tomato sauce to the saucepan with the garlic and onions. Simmer for 20 minutes. Add fresh basil at the end.

1 SERVING: CALORIES 110;FAT 5G; SODIUM 250MG; CARBOHYDRATES 12G; SUGAR 4G; FIBER 3G; PROTEIN 3G

NINJA KNOW-HOW YOU CAN SUBSTITUTE 8 RIPE ROMA TOMATOES, JUST SIMMER FOR TWO HOURS INSTEAD OF 20 MINUTES.

PREP TIME: 15 minutes   **SERVINGS:** 4   **CONTAINER:** 56-ounce Food Processor Bowl

wild sockeye salmon hand roll

A perfect alternative to sushi, filled with protein and extra nutrients from the parsley, ginger and avocado.

ingredients

1 celery stalk, cut into 1-inch chunks

2 tablespoons chopped red onion

¼ cup fresh parsley

½ cup pineapple

½ avocado, pitted, cut in thirds

1 teaspoon ground ginger

1 tablespoon tamari sauce

1 can (14.75 ounces) sockeye salmon, drained

12 sheets nori

1 cup mixed greens

directions

1. Place the celery, red onion, parsley, pineapple, avocado, ginger, tamari, and salmon into the 56-ounce Processor and hold the Auto-iQ™ PULSE button until desired chop.

2. Place the nori sheets on a flat surface and divide the salmon mixture evenly. Divide mixed greens evenly and roll to close forming a cone.

1 SERVING: CALORIES 235; FAT 53G; SODIUM 752MG; CARBOHYDRATES 9G; SUGAR 3G; FIBER 3G; PROTEIN 26G

 NINJA KNOW-HOW NORI SHEETS ARE FOUND IN ANY SUPERMARKET IN THE ETHNIC SECTION.

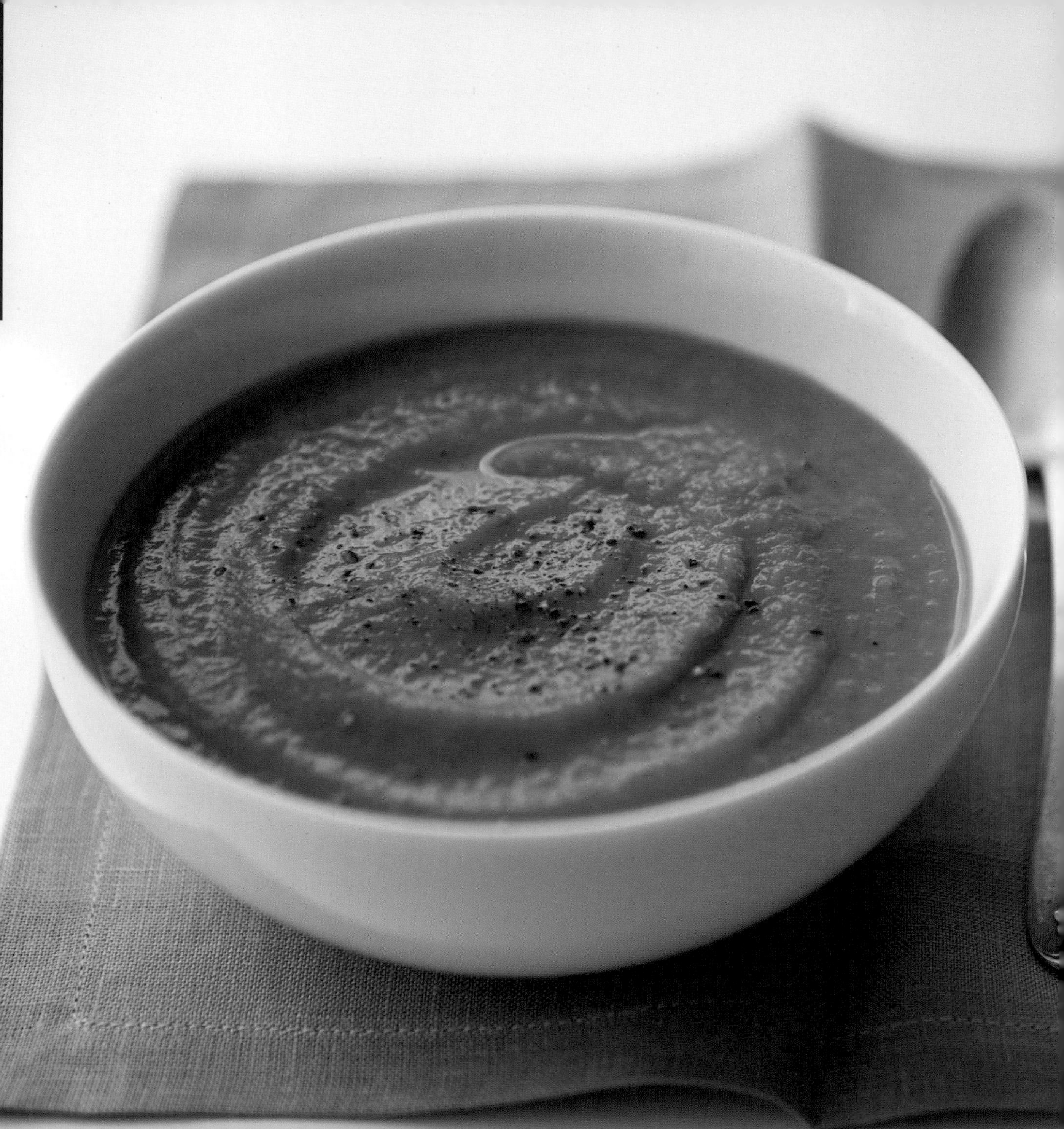

curried carrot soup

This delicious beta-carotene-rich carrot soup is fantastic with the added Indian flavor.

ingredients

2 teaspoons extra-virgin olive oil

3 cloves garlic, peeled, chopped

1 medium yellow onion, chopped

½ teaspoon kosher salt

½ teaspoon ground black pepper

1 tablespoon red curry paste

2 cups chopped carrots, peeled

4½ cups unsalted chicken broth

1 cup light coconut milk

directions

1. In a stockpot at medium-low heat, add the oil, garlic, and onions. Cook for 5 minutes.

2. Add the salt, black pepper, red curry paste, carrots, and chicken broth. Bring to a boil, reduce the heat to medium-low, and cook for 20–25 minutes or until the carrots are fork-tender.

3. Remove from the heat, add the coconut milk, and cool to room temperature.

4. Place mixture into the Pitcher. Turn unit ON, then select Auto-iQ™ PUREE. Blend until smooth.

5. Return to pot and simmer until heated.

1 SERVING: CALORIES 130; FAT 8G; SODIUM 570MG; CARBOHYDRATES 15G; SUGAR 7G; FIBER 4G; PROTEIN 1G

NINJA KNOW-HOW
SUBSTITUTE LOW-SODIUM CHICKEN BROTH IF YOU WANT TO REDUCE THE SALT.

PREP TIME: 10 minutes   COOK TIME: 15 minutes   SERVINGS: 2–4   CONTAINER: 72-ounce Pitcher

pep in your step soup

This recipe smells and tastes like summer.

ingredients

3 red bell peppers, roasted, peeled

¼ cup sun-dried tomatoes

2 cloves garlic, peeled

¼ cup white wine

¼ bunch Italian parsley, trimmed

1 cup low-sodium vegetable broth

salt and pepper to taste

balsamic vinegar, as garnish

directions

1. Place all of the ingredients into the Pitcher in the order listed.

2. Turn unit ON and select Auto-iQ™ PUREE.

3. Transfer to a medium saucepan and simmer until heated through, about 10 minutes. Serve hot in bowls garnished with a splash of balsamic vinegar, if desired.

1 SERVING: CALORIES 116; FAT 2G; SODIUM 204MG; CARBOHYDRATES 18G; SUGAR 7G; FIBER 7G; PROTEIN 3G

 NINJA KNOW-HOW : THIS SOUP CAN BE USED AS A DELICIOUS SAUCE FOR POULTRY OR SEAFOOD.

gazpacho

Gazpacho, a refreshing summertime soup, is packed full of flavor and nutrition! Add chilled cooked shrimp to transform it into a full meal!

ingredients

1 small red onion, peeled, cut in quarters

2 English cucumbers, cut in half and cut in quarters

1 yellow pepper, cut in quarters

1 red pepper, cut in quarters

3 pounds fresh tomatoes, peeled, seeded, and chopped

1 teaspoon garlic, minced

4 tablespoons red wine vinegar

3½ teaspoons kosher salt

48 ounces tomato juice

directions

1. Working in batches, add the red onion, cucumber, peppers, and fresh tomatoes to the Pitcher.

2. Turn unit ON, then hold down Auto-iQ™ PULSE until ingredients are finely chopped. Pour each batch into a large mixing bowl.

3. Add minced garlic, red wine vinegar, salt, and tomato juice and mix well.

4. Chill for at least 3 hours.

5. Taste for seasonings before serving.

1 SERVING: CALORIES 90; FAT 0G; SODIUM 1330MG; CARBOHYDRATES 19G; SUGAR 12G; FIBER 4G; PROTEIN 4G

NINJA KNOW-HOW : CHILL COVERED IN THE REFRIGERATOR OVERNIGHT TO DEVELOP AND MELD FLAVORS.

soups, sauces & entrées

kale & celery root soup

• •

This soup has only 60 calories per serving! It's also extremely nutrient-rich. Here's to your health!

ingredients

2 teaspoons extra-virgin olive oil

2 cloves garlic, peeled, chopped

1 medium yellow onion, chopped

1 cup chopped, peeled celery root

2 cups chopped kale

1½ teaspoons kosher salt

½ teaspoon ground black pepper

5 cups unsalted vegetable broth

directions

1. In a 5-quart saucepot at medium-low heat, add the oil, garlic, and onions. Cook for 6 minutes.

2. Add the remaining ingredients, bring to a boil, reduce the heat to medium-low, and cook for 20–25 minutes or until the celery root is fork-tender.

3. Remove from the heat and cool to room temperature.

4. Place mixture into the Pitcher. Turn unit ON. Select IQ-PUREE and blend until smooth.

5. Return to pot and simmer until heated.

1 SERVING: CALORIES 60; FAT 2G; SODIUM 720MG; CARBOHYDRATES 9G; SUGAR 3G; FIBER 2G; PROTEIN 2G

NINJA KNOW-HOW : ADD 1 TABLESPOON FLAXSEED FOR A SUPER FOOD BOOST.

PREP TIME: 10 minutes   COOK TIME: 35–40 minutes   SERVINGS: 8   CONTAINER: 72-ounce Pitcher

butternut squash soup with chicken sausage

This soup is absolutely delicious, full of root vegetables, with lean protein from the homemade chicken apple sausage.

ingredients

3 tablespoons olive oil

1 large yellow onion, chopped

1 cup raw cashews

1 large apple, peeled, cored, chopped

1 large carrot, peeled, chopped

2 pounds butternut squash, cubed

1 teaspoon fresh thyme leaves

1 bay leaf

4 cups vegetable stock, plus more to thin if desired

½ teaspoon kosher salt, plus more to taste

Black pepper, to taste

Chicken apple sausage (recipe page 101)

directions

1. Heat oil in a large saucepot and add the onions, cooking until they begin to soften, about 5 minutes. Add the cashews and cook, stirring, for about 5 minutes.

2. Add the chopped apple, carrot, squash, thyme, and bay leaf to the pot and cook for 5 minutes. Add the stock and stir to combine. Bring the soup to a boil and reduce the heat to medium-low, allowing to simmer until the squash is easily pierced with a knife, 20–25 minutes. Remove and discard bay leaf.

3. Allow soup to cool to room temperature. Working in batches, ladle the soup into the Pitcher. Turn unit ON and select Auto-iQ™ PUREE. Heat soup to desired temperature before serving. Top with crumbled chicken apple sausage.

1 SERVING: CALORIES 330; FAT 17G; SODIUM 590MG; CARBOHYDRATES 33G; SUGAR 13G; FIBER 5G; PROTEIN 16G

NINJA KNOW-HOW: FOR A VEGAN VERSION, ADD CANNELINI BEANS INSTEAD OF THE SAUSAGE.

PREP TIME: 20 minutes   COOK TIME: 25 minutes   SERVINGS: 4   CONTAINER: 72-ounce Pitcher

vegetable enchilada soup

Plantains, "potatoes of the air" or "cooking bananas," are the fruit of the Musa paradisiaca, a type of banana plant. In many countries they are consumed as a vegetable.

ingredients

½ medium yellow onion, cut in half

1 cup zucchini, cut into 1-inch chunks

1 can (10 ounces) mild enchilada sauce

2 tablespoons mild green chilies

1 tablespoon chili powder

1 teaspoon ground cumin

2 teaspoons dried oregano

1 cup fresh cilantro, stems removed

2 tablespoons vegetable oil

4 cups vegetable broth

¾ cup corn

½ cup plantains, cooked, cut into 1-inch pieces

1 can (15.5 ounces) pinto beans, drained

½ teaspoon kosher salt

½ teaspoon ground black pepper

¼ cup sliced black olives

⅓ cup shredded Mexican-blend cheese

directions

1. Place the onion and zucchini into the Pitcher. Turn unit ON. Hold down Auto-iQ™ PULSE until finely chopped. Remove mixture and set aside.

2. Place the enchilada sauce, chilies, chili powder, cumin, oregano, and cilantro into the Pitcher. Turn unit ON. Select MEDIUM and blend until smooth.

3. Heat oil in a stockpot and sauté onion and zucchini on medium heat until softened, about 8 minutes.

4. Add the pureed mixture, vegetable broth, corn, plantains, pinto beans, salt, and black pepper and bring to a boil. Reduce heat and simmer for 15 minutes, stirring occasionally.

5. To serve, ladle soup in a bowl and garnish each serving with black olives and cheese.

1 SERVING: CALORIES 360; FAT 13G; SODIUM 1740MG; CARBOHYDRATES 50G; SUGAR 13G; FIBER 5G; PROTEIN 14G

NINJA KNOW-HOW — REPLACE POTATOES WITH PLANTAINS IN YOUR FAVORITE VEGETABLE SOUP AND STEW RECIPES.

PREP TIME: 10 minutes   **COOK TIME:** 4–6 minutes   **SERVINGS:** 4   **CONTAINER:** 56-ounce Food Processor Bowl

salmon burgers

Salmon burgers are not only delicious, they are high in omega-3 oils. A healthier substitute for beef.

ingredients

1 pound boneless and skinless salmon, frozen for 30 minutes, cut into 1½-inch chunks

1½ teaspoons Dijon mustard

1 tablespoon lemon juice

1 egg, beaten

½ teaspoon salt

½ teaspoon black pepper

2 green onions, cut in half

¼ cup panko panko bread crumbs

2 teaspoons olive oil

directions

1. Add ¼ of the salmon, mustard, and lemon juice to the Food Processor Bowl. Turn unit ON, then hold down Auto-iQ™ PULSE for 5–10 pulses until finely chopped. Add the egg, salt, and pepper, then continue to hold down Auto-iQ™ PULSE for 3 additional pulses.

2. Add remaining salmon and green onions, then hold down Auto-iQ™ PULSE just until combined yet chunky, 2–3 pulses.

3. Remove salmon mixture and place in large bowl. Hand stir in the panko bread crumbs, then shape the mixture into four burgers.

4. In a nonstick sauté pan, heat oil over medium-high heat. Add salmon and cook until golden outside and cooked through, about 2–3 minutes per side. Serve on bun with lettuce, tomato, and red onion.

1 SERVING: CALORIES 190; FAT 8G; SODIUM 410MG; CARBOHYDRATES 5G; SUGAR 1G; FIBER 1G; PROTEIN 26G

NINJA KNOW-HOW   YOU MAY SUBSTITUTE CANNED RED SALMON FOR THE FRESH. YOU WILL NEED FEWER PULSES THAN WITH THE FROZEN CHUNKS.

pork chops with peach chutney

Peaches are an often-overlooked tasty combination with pork.

ingredients

½ medium onion

1 tablespoon ginger, peeled

½ jalapeño, seeded

1½ cups peaches, pitted, sliced

2 tablespoons lime juice

1 tablespoon agave nectar

2 teaspoons red wine vinegar

¼ teaspoon kosher salt

¼ teaspoon ground black pepper

⅓ teaspoon nutmeg

½ cup golden raisins

½ cup parsley leaves

4 pork chops, heated

directions

1. Place the onion, ginger, jalapeño, peaches, lime juice, agave nectar, vinegar, salt, black pepper, nutmeg, raisins, and parsley into the Food Processor Bowl and then hold down Auto-iQ™ PULSE until desired chop.

2. Place mixture into a saucepot and simmer for 20 minutes, stirring occasionally.

3. To serve, place one heated pork chop on a plate and top with the chutney.

1 SERVING: CALORIES 447; FAT 14G; SODIUM 228MG;
CARBOHYDRATES 29G; SUGAR 25G;
FIBER 2G; PROTEIN 48G

NINJA KNOW-HOW THIS CHUTNEY IS EQUALLY DELICIOUS SERVED WITH CHICKEN, AND TURKEY.

PREP TIME: 10 minutes   COOK TIME: 40–50 minutes   SERVINGS: 2–4   CONTAINER: 72-ounce Pitcher

butternut mac & cheese

Your kids will never suspect this macaroni and cheese is loaded with vegetables!

ingredients

1 pound butternut squash, peeled and cut into large pieces

1 cup water

1 cup low-fat milk

Salt and pepper to taste

1 teaspoon dry mustard powder

3 cups Cheddar cheese, shredded, divided

8 ounces elbow macaroni, cooked

¼ cup bread crumbs

¼ cup grated Parmesan cheese

2 teaspoons olive oil

directions

1. Place the squash into the Pitcher. Turn unit ON, then hold down Auto-iQ™ PULSE until roughly chopped.

2. In a saucepan, place the squash, water, milk, salt, pepper, and mustard. Simmer for 20 minutes. Add 2½ cups cheese and stir until melted. Cool to room temperature.

3. Add the cooled mixture to the Pitcher and select Auto-iQ™ PUREE.

4. Place cooked macaroni in a lightly buttered 2½-quart baking dish. Pour squash mixture over macaroni. Toss bread crumbs, remaining Cheddar cheese, Parmesan cheese, and oil and scatter over top.

5. Bake at 375°F for 20–25 minutes, until bubbly.

1 SERVING: CALORIES 470; FAT 24G; SODIUM 480MG; CARBOHYDRATES 42G; SUGAR 6G; FIBER 3G; PROTEIN 23G

NINJA KNOW-HOW | **USE LOW-FAT CHEDDAR CHEESE AND WHOLE WHEAT MACARONI AS HEALTHIER SWAPS.**

chicken pot pie

A classic favorite to make as a delicious comfort-food family meal.

ingredients

CRUST
(recipe page 199)

FILLING

4 carrots, peeled and cut into thirds

3 celery stalks, cut into thirds

1½ small onions, cut in quarters

1 pound boneless, skinless chicken breasts, approximately 2 breasts

2 tablespoons olive oil

8 tablespoons butter

8 tablespoons flour

4 cups chicken broth

1 tablespoon loosely packed thyme

Kosher salt and pepper

2 tablespoons milk

directions

1. FOR CRUST: See recipe directions on page 199.

2. FOR FILLING: Preheat oven to 375°F. Place carrots, celery, and onion into the Food Processor Bowl. Turn unit ON, then hold down Auto-iQ™ PULSE until coarsely chopped. Remove vegetables and set aside.

3. Place chicken into the Food Processor Bowl, then hold down Auto-iQ™ PULSE until chicken is chopped into bite-sized pieces.

4. Place a large skillet on stovetop set to medium heat and add chopped vegetables. Cook for 2–3 minutes. Add chopped chicken and continue cooking chicken and vegetables until vegetables are softened and chicken is cooked through, about 5–8 minutes.

5. Place a medium saucepan on stovetop set to medium heat. Melt butter and add flour, stirring constantly for 3 minutes. Add broth, stirring constantly with a whisk, until mixture thickens to form a sauce. Add thyme and season with salt and pepper.

6. Stir in desired amount of sauce to vegetables and chicken and pour into casserole dish. Remove crust from refrigerator and roll out to 2 inches larger than casserole dish. Place crust on top of filling and crimp as desired. Cut vent holes in crust and brush with milk. Cook for 45–50 minutes until crust is lightly browned.

1 SERVING: CALORIES 480; FAT 36G; SODIUM 920MG; CARBOHYDRATES 26G; SUGAR 3G; FIBER 2G; PROTEIN 15G

NINJA® KNOW-HOW — SAVE ON CALORIES AND MAKE WITHOUT THE CRUST AS A CASSEROLE OVER A BED OF KALE OR SPINACH.

mediterranean chicken salad

Simply delicious chicken salad that you can make in minutes.

ingredients

1 cup romaine lettuce, large chunks plus 3 whole romaine leaves

4 ounces chicken breast, precooked

½ cup cherry tomatoes

¼ cup kalamata olives

¼ cup feta cheese

directions

1. Place all of the ingredients into the Food Processor Bowl in the order listed.

2. Turn unit ON, then hold down Auto-iQ™ PULSE for 3 pulses or until desired chop is achieved.

1 SERVING: CALORIES 390; FAT 21G; SODIUM 910MG; CARBOHYDRATES 8G; SUGAR 4G; FIBER 2G; PROTEIN 4G

NINJA KNOW-HOW: SERVE ON ROMAINE LETTUCE LEAVES AS A LOW-CALORIE ALTERNATIVE TO A SANDWICH.

chicken pita sandwich

An easy, high-protein dinner in less than 30 minutes with scrumptious, ethnic flavors.

ingredients

1 pound raw chicken breast, cut into 2-inch pieces

¼ cup tandoori marinade (recipe page 120)

4 8-inch whole wheat pita bread rounds

3 vine-ripe tomatoes

8 Boston lettuce leaves

⅓ cup cucumber feta dip (optional see recipe on page 169)

directions

1. Marinate the chicken breast pieces for 2 hours.

2. Place the marinated chicken breast pieces into the Food Processor Bowl. Turn unit ON and hold down Auto-iQ™ PULSE until desired chop.

3. Lightly coat a nonstick skillet with cooking spray. Over medium heat, sauté the chicken mixture until cooked, about 4 minutes.

4. To assemble sandwich, cut pita bread rounds in half, open the pocket, place the lettuce and tomato in, and evenly divide the cucumber feta dip and cooked ground chicken into the pockets.

1 SERVING: CALORIES 340; FAT 4.5G; SODIUM 380MG; CARBOHYDRATES 40G; SUGAR 6G; FIBER 3G; PROTEIN 3G

 FOR A REAL LOW-CALORIE LUNCH, USE THE LETTUCE LEAVES AS YOUR WRAP AND LEAVE OUT THE PITA ROUNDS.

KNOW-HOW

PREP TIME: 15 minutes SERVINGS: 4 CONTAINER: 56-ounce Food Processor Bowl

healthy cobb salad

Dark green leafy mixed greens are, calorie for calorie, probably the most concentrated source of nutrition of any food. This tasty salad contains 11 grams of fiber and 34 grams of protein.

ingredients

¾ **pound cooked turkey breast, cut into cubes**

1 cup cubed beets, cooked

8 cups mixed greens

4 large hard-boiled eggs, cut in quarters

1 cup crumbled feta cheese

2 ripe avocados, pitted, chopped

2 oranges, peeled, chopped

directions

1. Place the turkey into the Food Processor Bowl. Turn unit ON and hold down Auto-iQ™ PULSE until desired chop. Remove turkey and set aside.

2. Place the beets into the Food Processor Bowl and hold down Auto-iQ™ PULSE until desired chop.

3. In a salad bowl, place the mixed greens and arrange each ingredient in a separate line.

4. Top with your favorite healthy salad dressing.

1 SERVING: CALORIES 480; FAT 28G; SODIUM 1640MG; CARBOHYDRATES 30G; SUGAR 14G; FIBER 11G; PROTEIN 34G

NINJA KNOW-HOW

TO GET MORE DARK GREEN LEAFY VEGETABLES IN YOUR SALADS, ADD WATERCRESS, FRESH BASIL, ROMAINE, GREEN LEAF, ARUGULA, AND BUTTERHEAD LETTUCE.

cauliflower couscous

Cauliflower and other cruciferous vegetables support our bodies' detox system.

ingredients

3 cups cauliflower, cut into 2-inch florets

1 tablespoon chopped rosemary, stems removed

1 clove garlic, chopped

2 teaspoons lemon juice

¼ cup extra-virgin olive oil

½ teaspoon kosher salt

½ teaspoon ground black pepper

½ cup sliced almonds

¼ cup sliced green onion

directions

1. Place the cauliflower into the Food Processor Bowl. Turn unit ON and hold down Auto-iQ™ PULSE until finely chopped.

2. In a stockpot, bring 3 quarts of water to a boil, then add the cauliflower. Cook until tender. Strain well.

3. Transfer cauliflower to a mixing bowl and add the rosemary, garlic, lemon juice, olive oil, salt, black pepper, almonds, and green onion. Toss to combine.

1 SERVING: CALORIES 211; FAT 20G; SODIUM 255MG; CARBOHYDRATES 8G; SUGAR 2G; FIBER 3G; PROTEIN 4G

 NINJA **KNOW-HOW** PULSE AND GENTLY CHOP WHOLE ALMONDS IN YOUR NINJA FOOD PROCESSOR BOWL IF YOU DON'T HAVE SLICED ALMONDS.

PREP TIME: 15 minutes   **COOK TIME:** 25 minutes   **SERVINGS:** 4   **CONTAINER:** 56-ounce Food Processor Bowl

stuffed flounder

This recipe will be a big hit with your familly, well worth the bit of extra work.

ingredients

½ medium onion, cut in 2-inch chunks

1 celery stalk, cut in 2-inch chunks

½ medium green bell pepper, cut in 2-inch chunks

1 clove garlic

1 pound shrimp, raw, peeled, deveined

¾ cup buttery crackers

1 tablespoon vegetable oil

1 tablespoon Dijon mustard

3 dashes hot sauce

2 teaspoons lemon juice

2 teaspoons Creole seasoning

1 tablespoon tomato paste

4 6-ounce flounder fillets

⅓ cup diced tomato

directions

1. Preheat oven to 350°F.

2. Place the onion, celery, green pepper, and garlic into the Food Processor Bowl. Turn unit ON. Hold down Auto-iQ™ PULSE until finely chopped. Remove mixture and set aside.

3. In the same Food Processor Bowl, place the shrimp and crackers and hold down Auto-iQ™ PULSE until finely chopped.

4. Heat oil in a saucepot and sauté vegetable mixture on medium heat for 5 minutes, stirring occasionally.

5. Place cooked vegetable mixture and shrimp mixture in a mixing bowl, then add the mustard, hot sauce, lemon juice, Creole seasoning, and tomato paste.

6. Lay flounder fillet flat on the prep area and add the stuffing mixture, then roll flounder to cover. Lightly coat a baking pan with cooking spray and arrange stuffed flounder on pan. Bake for 20 minutes or until flounder is cooked through.

1 SERVING: CALORIES 319; FAT 11G; SODIUM 1431MG; CARBOHYDRATES 14G; SUGAR 3G; FIBER 1G; PROTEIN 38G

NINJA KNOW-HOW: YOU CAN EASILY SUBSTITUTE TILAPIA FOR THE FLOUNDER.

coconut chicken in orange sauce

Light coconut milk is lower in calories, and gives a rich texture and nutty sweetness to this delicious dish.

ingredients

1 can (14 ounces) light coconut milk

2 cloves garlic

½ teaspoon kosher salt

2 tablespoons green curry paste

4 6-ounce chicken breasts

½ cup orange marmalade

2 tablespoons prepared horseradish

Cornstarch, to coat

¼ cup vegetable oil

directions

1. Place the coconut milk, garlic, salt, and curry paste into the Jumbo Multi-Serve 32-ounce Cup. Turn unit ON and select MEDIUM. Blend until smooth.

2. In an airtight container, place the chicken in the coconut mixture and marinate for 12 hours.

3. Preheat oven to 375°F.

4. In a mixing bowl, combine the marmalade and horseradish.

5. Remove chicken and drain excess marinade. Coat chicken in cornstarch.

6. In a nonstick sauté pan, heat the oil over medium-high heat. Add the chicken, then cook for 2 minutes per side. Remove chicken and place on lined sheet pan that has been lightly coated with cooking spray. Bake for 10 minutes or until thoroughly cooked through.

7. Place chicken on a plate and serve with a side of the marmalade horseradish sauce.

1 SERVING: CALORIES 520; FAT 26G; SODIUM 500MG; CARBOHYDRATES 36G; SUGAR 27G; FIBER 2G; PROTEIN 37G

NINJA KNOW-HOW — A CHICKEN BREAST DROPS DOWN TO 19% FAT WHEN SKINNED COMPARED WITH 36% WITH SKIN.

PREP TIME: 15 minutes   **SERVINGS:** 4   **CONTAINER:** 56-ounce Food Processor Bowl

chopped salad with garbanzo beans

The mushrooms in this salad are a rich source of selenium and umami, which makes food more flavorful.

ingredients

1 can (15.5 ounces) whole black medium olives, drained

½ red bell pepper, seeded, cut into 1-inch chunks

1 cup button mushrooms

1 cup English cucumber, cut into 1-inch chunks

4 small radishes, tops removed, cut in half

8 cups chopped romaine lettuce

1 can (15.5 ounces) garbanzo beans, drained

4 tablespoons sunflower seeds

directions

1. Place the black olives, red pepper, mushrooms, cucumber, and radish into the Food Processor Bowl.

2. Turn unit ON and select Auto-iQ™ PULSE until desired chop.

3. In a salad bowl place the lettuce and top with the vegetable mixture, garbanzo beans and sunflower seeds.

4. Top with your favorite healthy salad dressing.

1 SERVING: CALORIES 280; FAT 13G; SODIUM 590MG; CARBOHYDRATES 35G; SUGAR 3G; FIBER 5G; PROTEIN 12G

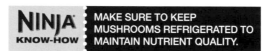

NINJA KNOW-HOW   MAKE SURE TO KEEP MUSHROOMS REFRIGERATED TO MAINTAIN NUTRIENT QUALITY.

PREP TIME: 10 minutes   COOK TIME: 15 minutes   SERVINGS: 2–4   CONTAINER: 56-ounce Food Processor Bowl

turkey meatballs

Meatballs are fun and easy to make when you have a Ninja food processor. They always taste better homemade.

ingredients

1 pound dark turkey meat, cut into 1-inch cubes and well-chilled

½ onion, peeled, chopped

4 cloves garlic, peeled and minced

¼ cup chopped Italian parsley

½ cup grated Parmesan cheese

¼ cup bread crumbs

2 tablespoons tomato paste

2 eggs, beaten

Salt and pepper to taste

Cooking spray

4 cups sun-dried tomato sauce (recipe page 122)

directions

1. Add the turkey to the Food Processor Bowl. Turn unit ON, then hold down Auto-iQ™ PULSE until turkey is finely chopped. Do not overprocess.

2. Transfer the turkey to a bowl and add onion, garlic, parsley, Parmesan cheese, bread crumbs, tomato paste, egg, salt, and pepper, mixing to combine. Form mixture into mini meatballs.

3. Lightly coat a large skillet with cooking spray. Over medium-high heat, sauté meatballs until browned on all sides, about 5 minutes. Add marinara sauce and simmer until sauce is thickened and meatballs are cooked through completely, about 15–20 minutes.

1 SERVING: CALORIES 500; FAT 22G; SODIUM 940MG; CARBOHYDRATES 33G; SUGAR 11G; FIBER 7G; PROTEIN 38G

NINJA KNOW-HOW   YOU CAN SUBSTITUTE CHICKEN FOR THE TURKEY IN THIS RECIPE.

PREP TIME: 15 minutes COOK TIME: 8 minutes SERVINGS: 4 CONTAINER: 56-ounce Food Processor Bowl

lamb chops with pistachio tapenade

Pistachios are one of the lowest-calorie nuts and have a sweet and savory taste, perfect with rich meats.

ingredients

1 cup pistachios, shelled

½ cup green olives

2 tablespoons capers

2 cloves garlic

2 tablespoons red wine vinegar

3 tablespoons extra-virgin olive oil

¼ cup chopped fresh basil

2 teaspoons Dijon mustard

¼ teaspoon ground black pepper

1 tablespoon olive oil

12 lamb chops

directions

1. Place the pistachios, olives, capers, garlic, vinegar, olive oil, basil, mustard, and black pepper into the Food Processor Bowl and hold down Auto-iQ™ PULSE until desired chop, scraping sides as needed.

2. In a nonstick sauté pan, heat the olive oil over medium-high heat. Season lamb with salt and black pepper and then place the lamb chops in the pan and sauté until browned on both sides and heated to desired temperature, about 6–8 minutes.

3. To serve, place three chops on a plate and top with the tapenade.

1 SERVING: CALORIES 600; FAT 42G; SODIUM 540MG; CARBOHYDRATES 11G; SUGAR 3G; FIBER 4G; PROTEIN 48G

NINJA KNOW-HOW
EXCLUSIVELY PASTURE-FED LAMB HAS THE HIGHEST NUTRITIONAL VALUE.

PREP TIME: 15 minutes   COOK TIME: 12 minutes   SERVINGS: 8   CONTAINER: 56-ounce Food Processor Bowl

black bean fiesta burger

Unlike canned vegetables, which have lost much of their nutritional value, there is little difference in the nutritional value between canned beans and those you cook yourself. This recipe contains 14 grams of fiber and 17 grams of protein.

ingredients

2 cans (15½ ounces) black beans, drained

½ medium onion

2 cloves garlic

1 large egg, beaten

1 cup quinoa, cooked

1 lime, juiced

2 tablespoons ground cumin

¾ cup fresh cilantro

⅔ cup textured vegetable protein, rehydrated

½ cup gluten-free bread crumbs

½ teaspoon kosher salt

½ teaspoon ground black pepper

directions

1. Place the black beans, onion, garlic, and egg into the Food Processor Bowl. Turn unit ON and hold down Auto-iQ™ PULSE until desired chop.

2. Transfer chopped ingredients to a mixing bowl and then add the quinoa, lime juice, cumin, cilantro, vegetable protein, bread crumbs, salt, and black pepper, mixing to combine. Form mixture into eight burgers.

3. Lightly coat a large skillet with cooking spray. Over medium-high heat, sauté burgers until browned on both sides and heated through, about 12 minutes.

1 SERVING: CALORIES 250; FAT 3G; SODIUM 600MG; CARBOHYDRATES 40G; SUGAR 2G; FIBER 14G; PROTEIN 17G

NINJA KNOW-HOW FOR AN UNEXPECTED SWEET FLAVOR, ADD 1 TABLESPOON BALSAMIC VINEGAR TO THE RECIPE.

PREP TIME: 20 minutes **COOK TIME:** 40 minutes **SERVINGS:** 6 **CONTAINER:** 56-ounce Food Processor Bowl

cheeseburger stew

This stew is a hearty one-pot meal, perfect for an easy weekday meal.

ingredients

1½ **pounds lean ground beef, cut into 2-inch cubes**

½ **medium yellow onion, chopped**

1 **celery stalk, chopped**

1 **carrot, peeled, chopped**

3 **tablespoons butter**

3 **tablespoons all-purpose flour**

3 **cups low-sodium beef broth**

1 **cup low-fat milk**

1½ **cups Idaho potatoes, peeled, cut into 1-inch pieces**

1 **tablespoon dried oregano**

2 **tablespoons Worcestershire sauce**

½ **teaspoon kosher salt**

¾ **teaspoon ground black pepper**

⅓ **cup shredded low-fat Cheddar cheese**

⅓ **cup diced tomato**

directions

1. Place the beef, onion, celery, and carrot into the Food Processor Bowl. Turn unit ON and hold down Auto-iQ™ PULSE until finely chopped.

2. In a stockpot, heat butter over medium-high heat. Add the beef and vegetable mixture and cook until vegetables are softened, about 8–10 minutes.

3. Add the flour, stirring to combine, and cook for 1 minute.

4. Add the beef broth, milk, potatoes, oregano, Worcestershire, salt, and black pepper and bring to a boil. Reduce heat and simmer for about 15 minutes or until potatoes are fork-tender, stirring occasionally.

5. To serve, ladle soup in a bowl and garnish each serving with cheese and tomato.

1 SERVING: CALORIES 380; FAT 21G; SODIUM 446MG; CARBOHYDRATES 17G; SUGAR 5G; FIBER 2G; PROTEIN 30G

NINJA KNOW-HOW USE CELERY LEAVES FOR ADDED NUTRIENTS AND TASTE.

PREP TIME: 10 minutes **COOK TIME:** 35 minutes **SERVINGS:** 6 **CONTAINER:** 56-ounce Food Processor Bowl

barbecue turkey shepherd's pie

This tasty recipe is a well-balanced complete meal with only 320 calories per serving and a great meal for using leftover chicken or turkey.

ingredients

2 cloves garlic

1 celery stalk

1 medium carrot, peeled

½ medium onion

2 tablespoons vegetable oil

2 tablespoons flour

1 cup low-sodium turkey broth, heated

1 cup barbecue sauce

¼ teaspoon kosher salt

¾ teaspoon ground black pepper

1½ pounds turkey breast, cooked, diced

1¼ cups frozen peas, thawed

3 cups mashed potatoes, heated

directions

1. Preheat oven to 375°F.

2. Place the garlic, celery, carrot, and onion into the Food Processor Bowl and hold down Auto-iQ™ PULSE until desired chop.

3. Heat oil in a stockpot and add vegetable mixture and sauté on medium heat until softened, about 7 minutes.

4. Add the flour, stirring to coat the vegetables.

5. Slowly whisk in the broth, then add the barbecue sauce, salt, black pepper, and turkey. Cook for 10 minutes or until heated. Stir in peas.

6. Pour mixture into a 9 x 9 baking dish and spread the mashed potatoes on top to cover turkey mixture. Bake for 30 minutes or until heated through.

1 SERVING: CALORIES 320; FAT 6G; SODIUM 2030MG; CARBOHYDRATES 44G; SUGAR 16G; FIBER 3G; PROTEIN 27G

NINJA **KNOW-HOW** | USE FREE-RANGE TURKEY FOR EVEN GREATER NUTRITION.

PREP TIME: 10 minutes **COOK TIME:** 6 minutes **SERVINGS:** 4 **CONTAINER:** 72-ounce Pitcher

beer-battered chicken tenderloins

· ·

The carbonation in the beer adds body and lightness to the batter. Depending on the type and quality, beer may also add color and flavor.

ingredients

2 quarts oil for deep-frying

¾ cup flour

1 large egg

2 teaspoons garlic powder

½ cup mini hard pretzels

½ teaspoon kosher salt

¼ teaspoon ground black pepper

1 bottle (12 ounces) light beer

1 pound chicken tenderloins

directions

1. Heat oil in a stockpot to 365°F.

2. Place the flour, egg, garlic powder, pretzels, salt, black pepper, and beer into the Pitcher. Turn unit ON and select MEDIUM. Blend until smooth, then pour mixture into a mixing bowl.

3. One at a time, dip the chicken tenders into the batter to coat, then place carefully into the hot oil. Fry until golden brown and cooked through, about 5 minutes. Remove chicken with slotted spoon and drain on a paper towel. Serve hot.

1 SERVING: CALORIES 470; FAT 23G; SODIUM 570MG; CARBOHYDRATES 31G; SUGAR 1G; FIBER 1G; PROTEIN 30G

NINJA KNOW-HOW | THE BEER OR SELTZER TEMPERATURE SHOULD BE COLD, WHICH HELPS MAKE THE BATTER CRISP.

PREP TIME: 15 minutes   COOK TIME: 25 minutes   SERVINGS: 8   CONTAINER: 56-ounce Food Processor Bowl

asian pork meatballs

Pork tenderloin is a great low-fat alternative for meats—only 2.5 grams of fat in these meatballs.

ingredients

1 pound pork tenderloin, cut into cubes

2 cloves garlic

2 tablespoons chopped fresh ginger, peeled

½ cup chopped scallions

2 tablespoons low-sodium soy sauce

1 teaspoon coriander

1 large egg

1 lime, juiced

¼ cup chopped pineapple

1 tablespoon whole-grain mustard

½ cup unseasoned bread crumbs

2 cups sweet and sour sauce, store-bought, warmed

½ cup chopped scallions

directions

1. Preheat oven to 350°F.

2. Place the pork, garlic, ginger, scallion, soy sauce, coriander, egg, lime juice, pineapple, mustard, and bread crumbs into the Food Processor Bowl. Turn unit ON and hold down Auto-iQ™ PULSE until desired chop.

3. Form into small meatballs. Bake on a sheet pan for 15 minutes or until cooked.

4. Toss meatballs with the warm sweet and sour sauce. Garnish with scallions.

1 SERVING: CALORIES 220; FAT 2.5G; SODIUM 500MG; CARBOHYDRATES 35G; SUGAR 15G; FIBER 1G; PROTEIN 15G

NINJA® KNOW-HOW | SERVE OVER A BED OF SPINACH OR QUINOA FOR A HEALTHY MEAL.

Spinach & Artichoke Dip, 164

CHAPTER 5:

entertaining

entertaining

tabbouleh dip

• •

This dip contains parsley, a culinary herb with the same amount of vitamin C as an orange. Plus, it's gluten-free!

ingredients

½ cup English cucumber, cut in quarters

¼ small yellow onion, peeled, cut in quarters

2 tablespoons fresh mint, stems removed

½ cup loosely packed flat-leaf parsley, stems removed

1½ vine-ripe tomatoes, chopped

¼ teaspoon ground black pepper

¼ teaspoon kosher salt

1 tablespoon extra-virgin olive oil

1 tablespoon freshly squeezed lemon juice

directions

1. Place all of the ingredients into the Small 18-ounce Cup in the order listed.

2. Turn unit ON, select Auto-iQ™ PULSE, and pulse until desired consistency is reached.

1 SERVING: CALORIES 30; FAT 2.5G; SODIUM 85MG; CARBOHYDRATES 2G; SUGAR 1G; FIBER 1G; PROTEIN 1G

NINJA
KNOW-HOW

SERVE THIS AS AN ACCOMPANIMENT TO GRILLED FISH, BEEF, OR LAMB.

PREP TIME: 5 minutes   SERVINGS: 2½ cups   CONTAINER: 56-ounce Food Processor Bowl

classic hummus

Adding roasted red peppers, olives, or roasted garlic will give this recipe your own personal twist. Enjoy with homemade pita chips or fresh vegetable crudités for an entertaining favorite!

ingredients

2 cups cooked, drained garbanzo beans (liquid reserved)

¼ cup plus 2 tablespoons garbanzo bean liquid

¼ cup lemon juice

¼ cup olive oil

1 garlic clove, peeled

1 teaspoon ground cumin

1/8 teaspoon cayenne pepper

1 teaspoon kosher salt

¼ teaspoon black pepper

directions

1. Place all of the ingredients into the Food Processor Bowl in the order listed.

2. Turn unit ON, then select Auto-iQ™ PUREE.

1 SERVING: CALORIES 52; FAT 3G; SODIUM 98MG; CARBOHYDRATES 5G; SUGAR 1G; FIBER 1G; PROTEIN 1G

NINJA **KNOW-HOW** FOR AN ULTRA SMOOTH HUMMUS, YOU CAN MAKE THIS RECIPE IN THE REGULAR 24-OUNCE CUP.

entertaining

spinach & artichoke dip

Delicious served with pita or whole-grain chips.

ingredients

¼ cup mayonnaise

¼ cup sour cream

8 ounces cream cheese

2 tablespoons lemon juice

1 can (14 ounces) artichoke hearts, drained and chopped

½ cup shredded low-fat mozzarella cheese

¼ cup Parmesan cheese, cut into pieces or grated

2 tablespoons chopped onion

1 cup frozen spinach, thawed, excess liquid removed

directions

1. Preheat oven to 350°F. Place all of the ingredients, except the spinach, into the Pitcher in the order listed. Turn unit ON, then hold down Auto-iQ™ PULSE until ingredients are combined.

2. Add the chopped spinach and continue to hold down Auto-iQ™ PULSE until incorporated. Spoon the dip into a heat-resistant serving dish and bake for 20 minutes. Serve with sliced French bread. Season with salt and pepper.

1 SERVING: CALORIES 30; FAT 2.5G; SODIUM 70MG; CARBOHYDRATES 1G; SUGAR 0G; FIBER 0G; PROTEIN 1G

 NINJA KNOW-HOW SUBSTITUTE LOW-FAT MAYONNAISE AND CREAM CHEESE FOR LOWER FAT CONTENT.

fruit salsa

Fresh salsa is a delicious low-calorie condiment choice, made with fruits, herbs and vegetables. Perfect to add to grilled chicken, morning eggs, and even your lunch sandwiches.

ingredients

1 small shallot, peeled

1 tablespoon pickled ginger

2 tablespoons raspberry vinegar

2 tablespoons sugar

½ cup fresh cilantro

½ lime, peeled

2 tablespoons water

½ teaspoon kosher salt

¼ teaspoon ground black pepper

1 cup chopped pineapple, peeled

1 cup chopped mango, peeled

directions

1. Place the shallot, ginger, vinegar, sugar, cilantro, lime, water, salt, and black pepper into the Food Processor Bowl. Turn unit ON and select Auto-iQ™ PUREE.

2. Add the pineapple, mango, and kiwi and hold down Auto-iQ™ PULSE until desired chop.

1 SERVING: CALORIES 15; FAT 0G; SODIUM 45MG; CARBOHYDRATES 4G; SUGAR 3G; FIBER 0G; PROTEIN 0G

 KNOW-HOW VARY SALSA BY ADDING A FRUIT LIKE PEACHES OR EVEN ADD BLACK BEANS.

chorizo taco dip

Extremely rich and delicious, even using the low-fat cream cheese.

ingredients

- 1 pound chorizo, chopped
- ½ medium onion
- 1 green bell pepper, seeded, chopped
- 1 tablespoon vegetable oil
- 1 package (8 ounces) low-fat cream cheese
- ½ cup low-fat ranch dressing
- 1 cup salsa
- 1 cup shredded Colby Jack cheese
- 1 package (1 ounce) low-sodium taco seasoning
- 1 cup sliced black olives

directions

1. Preheat oven to 350°F.

2. Place the chorizo, onion, and green pepper into the Food Processor Bowl. Turn unit ON and then hold down Auto-iQ™ PULSE until desired chop.

3. Heat oil in a stockpot and sauté mixture on medium-high heat until vegetables are tender, stirring occasionally. Place mixture into a mixing bowl.

4. Place the cream cheese, ranch dressing, salsa, cheese, and taco seasoning into the Food Processor Bowl and select MEDIUM. Blend until smooth.

5. Add the cream cheese mixture and black olives to the chorizo mixture, stirring to combine.

6. Place mixture into a 9 x 9 baking dish. Bake for 25 minutes or until hot.

1 SERVING: CALORIES 370; FAT 29G;
SODIUM 1090MG; CARBOHYDRATES 10G;
SUGAR 3G; FIBER 1G; PROTEIN 16G

NINJA KNOW-HOW | SUBSTITUTE CHICKEN SAUSAGE FOR A LOWER-FAT AND CALORIES.

entertaining

PREP TIME: 5 minutes   SERVINGS: 10–12   CONTAINER: 72-ounce Pitcher

fire-roasted tomato salsa

You can depend on the flavor of this salsa every time! Canned tomatoes create consistency and rich flavor.

ingredients

2 cans (10 ounces each) tomatoes

1 white onion, cut in quarters, peeled

1 jalapeño pepper, seeded

1 canned chipotle chile pepper, with 2 tablespoons adobo sauce

1 bunch fresh cilantro, stems trimmed

1 lime, peeled, cut in quarters

Salt and pepper to taste

directions

1. Add all of the ingredients to the Pitcher in the order listed.

2. Hold down Auto-iQ™ PULSE until desired consistency is achieved. Cover and refrigerate for at least 1 hour before serving.

1 SERVING: CALORIES 30; FAT 0G; SODIUM 220MG; CARBOHYDRATES 7G; SUGAR 3G; FIBER 2G; PROTEIN 1G

NINJA KNOW-HOW — YOU CAN MAKE A FRESH VERSION OF THIS BY SUBSTITUTING 10 OUNCES OF FRESH TOMATOES.

cucumber feta dip

A delicious and light dip perfect with fresh carrots, peppers, and celery sticks!

ingredients

¼ small red onion, cut in half

1 cup English cucumber, peeled and roughly chopped

¼ cup loosely packed fresh dill

½ cup crumbled feta cheese

1 tablespoon freshly squeezed lemon juice

¼ teaspoon ground black pepper

directions

1. Place ½ cup cucumber into the Small 18-ounce Cup, then add the rest of the ingredients in the order listed, finishing with the other half of the cucumber. Turn unit ON and select Auto-iQ™ PULSE for 8-10 pulses.

1 SERVING: CALORIES 60; FAT 4G; SODIUM 210MG; CARBOHYDRATES 2G; SUGAR 1G; FIBER 0G; PROTEIN 3G

NINJA KNOW-HOW
ADD ¼ CUP CELERY TOPS AND LEAVES FOR EXTRA CRUNCH AND NUTRIENTS.

curry bloody mary

· ·

Using fresh vegetables and Far Eastern spices makes this a delicious choice versus store mixes.

ingredients

2 small celery stalks,
1-inch chunks, plus extra
stalk for garnish

1 lemon, peeled, seeded

4 small vine-ripe tomatoes,
cut in quarters

1 cup carrot juice

2 teaspoons green curry
paste

1 teaspoon tamarind
concentrate

4 dashes hot sauce

Small pinch celery seed

4 ounces vodka

4 cups ice

directions

1. Place all of the ingredients, except the ice, into the Pitcher in the order listed.

2. Turn unit ON, then select Auto-iQ™ FROZEN DRINKS/SMOOTHIES.

3. Serve over ice and garnish with celery stalk.

1 SERVING: CALORIES 130; FAT 1G; SODIUM 70MG; CARBOHYDRATES 12G; SUGAR 7G; FIBER 2G; PROTEIN 1G

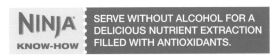

NINJA KNOW-HOW | SERVE WITHOUT ALCOHOL FOR A DELICIOUS NUTRIENT EXTRACTION FILLED WITH ANTIOXIDANTS.

entertaining

PREP TIME: 10 minutes   SERVINGS: 6   CONTAINER: 72-ounce Pitcher

watermelon basil sangria

A fresh summery cocktail is an excellent choice for your family barbecue.

ingredients

3 cups watermelon, cut in 1-inch chunks

¼ cup fresh basil, stems removed

2 limes, peeled, cut in half

1 cup frozen peaches

½ cup brandy

1 cup dry white wine

3 tablespoons agave nectar

2¼ cups ice

directions

1. Place all of the ingredients into the Pitcher in the order listed.

2. Turn unit ON, then select Auto-iQ™ FROZEN DRINKS/SMOOTHIES.

1 SERVING: CALORIES 150; FAT 0G; SODIUM 5MG; CARBOHYDRATES 20G; SUGAR 17G; FIBER 1G; PROTEIN 1G

 NINJA KNOW-HOW — MAKE THIS FRUITY DRINK WITH SPARKLING CIDER INSTEAD OF BRANDY AND WHITE WINE AS A GREAT FAMILY REFRESHER.

blueberry honey cucumber mojito

Fresh blueberries and cucumber create a refreshing cocktail, plus the calories are less than most popular frozen drinks.

ingredients

2½ cups fresh blueberries

1 cup chopped English cucumber

2 tablespoons fresh mint, stems removed

2 tablespoons honey

1 cup light rum

¾ cup pear juice

3 cups ice

directions

1. Place all of the ingredients into the Pitcher in the order listed.

2. Turn unit ON, then select Auto-iQ™ FROZEN DRINKS/SMOOTHIES.

1 SERVING: CALORIES 170; FAT 0G; SODIUM 5MG; CARBOHYDRATES 20G; SUGAR 15G; FIBER 2G; PROTEIN 1G

NINJA KNOW-HOW   ADD 1 TEASPOON FRESH GINGER FOR A SUPER FOOD BOOST.

PREP TIME: 5 minutes   SERVINGS: 4   CONTAINER: 72-ounce Pitcher

lem-mosa

A fresh delicious citrus cooler perfect as a palate cleanser.

ingredients

3 lemons, peeled, cut in half

2 tablespoons fresh mint, stems removed

1¾ cups sparkling wine

2 tablespoons agave nectar

3½ cups ice

directions

1. Place all of the ingredients into the Pitcher in the order listed.

2. Turn unit ON, then select Auto-iQ™ FROZEN DRINKS/SMOOTHIES.

1 SERVING: CALORIES 120; FAT 0G; SODIUM 5MG; CARBOHYDRATES 15G; SUGAR 9G; FIBER 1G; PROTEIN 1G

 NINJA KNOW-HOW   ADD FRESH RASPBERRIES AS A GARNISH OR BLEND FOR A NEW TWIST.

PREP TIME: 10 minutes   SERVINGS: 4   CONTAINER: 72-ounce Pitcher

strawberry daiquiri

Fresh strawberrries provide the natural sweetness to this cocktail.

ingredients

2 cups ice

4 cups strawberries, hulled,
cut in half

8 ounces lime juice

8 ounces light rum

directions

1. Place all of the ingredients in the Pitcher in the order listed.

2. Turn unit ON, then select Auto-iQ™ FROZEN DRINKS/SMOOTHIES.

1 SERVING: CALORIES 200; FAT 0G; SODIUM 5MG; CARBOHYDRATES 17G; SUGAR 8G;
FIBER 3G; PROTEIN 1G

NINJA KNOW-HOW — IF YOU WANT TO ADD A TOUCH OF SWEETNESS, ADD A FEW GRAPES TO KEEP IT NATURAL.

banana colada

Frozen pineapple, bananas and coconut milk make this indulgent cocktail fresh and delicious.

ingredients

2 cups frozen pineapple, 1-inch chunks

2 small bananas, peeled, frozen

8 ounces light rum

2 cups pineapple juice

1 cup light coconut milk

1 cup ice

directions

1. Place all of the ingredients into the Pitcher in the order listed.

2. Turn unit ON, then select Auto-iQ™ FROZEN DRINKS/SMOOTHIES.

1 SERVING: CALORIES 325; FAT 3G; SODIUM 25MG; CARBOHYDRATES 42G; SUGAR 27G; FIBER 4G; PROTEIN 2G

NINJA KNOW-HOW — TRY ADDING OTHER FRUITS SUCH AS FROZEN MANGO, STRAWBERRIES AND RASPBERRIES.

PREP TIME: 10 minutes   SERVINGS: 4   CONTAINER: 72-ounce Pitcher

pear ginger sake martini

Spicy and sweet flavors explode in this exotic cocktail.

ingredients

1 frozen pear, peeled, cored

½ teaspoon grated fresh ginger

2 cups pear juice

½ to ¾ cup sake

1 tablespoon agave nectar

1 cup ice

Crystallized ginger pieces, slit partway through

directions

1. Place all of the ingredients, except for the crystallized ginger, into the Pitcher in the order listed.

2. Turn unit ON, then select Auto-iQ™ FROZEN DRINKS/SMOOTHIES.

3. Pour into four chilled martini glasses and garnish with a piece of crystallized ginger.

1 SERVING: CALORIES 170; FAT 0G; SODIUM 10MG; CARBOHYDRATES 34G; SUGAR 24G; FIBER 1G; PROTEIN 0G

NINJA KNOW-HOW SERVE WITHOUT ALCOHOL AS A DETOX SPLASH OR ADD A LITTLE LEMON FOR EXTRA FLAVOR.

fresh citrus margarita

Using citrus fruit makes this classic drink taste fresher and controls the calories!

ingredients

1 lime, peeled, cut in half

1 lemon, peeled,
cut in quarters

⅓ cup orange juice

¼ cup triple sec

⅔ cup tequila

4 cups ice

directions

1. Place all of the ingredients into the Pitcher in the order listed.

2. Turn unit ON, then select Auto-iQ™ FROZEN DRINKS/SMOOTHIES.

1 SERVING: CALORIES 170; FAT 0G; SODIUM 5MG; CARBOHYDRATES 11G; SUGAR 8G; FIBER 1G; PROTEIN 0G

NINJA KNOW-HOW ADD WATERMELON OR BERRIES TO ADD A VARIETY OF FLAVORS TO THIS MARGARITA.

entertaining

PREP TIME: 10 minutes   SERVINGS: 4   CONTAINER: 72-ounce Pitcher

strawberry jalapeño margarita

Adding jalapeño gives a new spicy twist to a classic favorite.

ingredients

6 ounces blanco tequila

3 ounces freshly squeezed lime juice

4 cups frozen strawberries

4 teaspoons fresh jalapeño without seeds

2 cups ice

directions

1. Place all of the ingredients into the Pitcher in the order listed.

2. Turn unit ON, then select Auto-iQ™ FROZEN DRINKS/SMOOTHIES.

1 SERVING: CALORIES 230; FAT 0G; SODIUM 30MG; CARBOHYDRATES 22G; SUGAR 13G; FIBER 3G; PROTEIN 1G

NINJA KNOW-HOW   INSTEAD OF FRESHLY SQUEEZED LIME JUICE, ADD 2 PEELED WHOLE LIMES FOR ADDED FIBER.

PREP TIME: 10 minutes   SERVINGS: 4   CONTAINER: 72-ounce Pitcher

cool as a cucumber

· ·

If you have never tried a cucumber-based cocktail, you are going to be in for a especially cool surprise.

ingredients

3 ounces London dry gin

1 cup fresh cucumber (about 3 inches, peeled)

4 mint leaves

2 ounces freshly squeezed lime or lemon juice

2 ounce simple syrup or 1 ounce raw agave nectar

2 cups ice

directions

1. Place all of the ingredients into the Pitcher in the order listed.

2. Turn unit ON, then select Auto-iQ™ FROZEN DRINKS/SMOOTHIES.

1 SERVING: CALORIES 200; FAT 0G; SODIUM 10MG; CARBOHYDRATES 22G; SUGAR 18G; FIBER 1G; PROTEIN 1G

 KNOW-HOW ADD FOUR FRESH STRAWBERRIES FOR A TASTY AND COLORFUL VARIATION.

Peach Muffins, 194

CHAPTER 6:

breads & baked goods

PREP TIME: 10 minutes   BAKE TIME: 10–12 minutes   SERVINGS: 16 cookies   CONTAINER: 56-ounce Food Processor Bowl

gluten-free cranberry almond cookies

These cookies are so chewy and delicious—the coconut oil adds a nutty flavor and great taste.

ingredients

½ cup coconut oil

1 egg

½ teaspoon vanilla extract

½ cup packed brown sugar

½ cup granulated sugar

1¼ cups King Arthur gluten-free flour blend

½ cup almond meal

½ cup gluten-free oats

¼ cup shredded unsweetened coconut

¼ teaspoon baking soda

1 teaspoon kosher salt

½ teaspoon ground cinnamon

½ cup dried cranberries

directions

1. Preheat oven to 350°F.

2. Using the dough blade, add the coconut oil, egg, vanilla, brown sugar, and granulated sugar to the Food Processor Bowl. Turn unit ON, then hold down Auto-iQ™ PULSE for 3 pulses. Select MEDIUM and blend for 15 seconds to cream together the ingredients. Scrape down the sides.

3. In a medium bowl, combine the flour, almond meal, oats, coconut, baking soda, salt, and cinnamon. Stir to combine. Add half of the dry mix to the Food Processor Bowl. Hold down Auto-iQ™ PULSE for 3 pulses, then select MEDIUM and blend for 10 seconds. Scrape down the sides, then add remaining dry mix. Select MEDIUM and continue to blend for another 15 seconds until dough is evenly combined.

4. Add the cranberries to the Food Processor Bowl and hold down Auto-iQ™ PULSE until cranberries are evenly dispersed throughout.

5. Spoon tablespoon-sized cookie dough onto parchment-lined cookie sheets, about 2 inches apart. Bake for 10–12 minutes until JUST golden. Cookies will be very soft upon oven removal but will set within 5 minutes of resting.

1 SERVING: CALORIES 210; FAT 10G; SODIUM 150MG; CARBOHYDRATES 29G; SUGAR 16G; FIBER 1G; PROTEIN 3G

NINJA KNOW-HOW

IF YOU DON'T NEED TO EAT GLUTEN FREE, JUST SUBSTITUTE REGULAR FLOUR AND REGULAR OATS.

PREP TIME: 20 minutes   COOK TIME: 40 minutes   SERVINGS: 10–12   CONTAINER: 56-ounce Food Processor Bowl

cheddar jalapeño corn bread

A spicy twist to traditional corn bread makes it a great complement to your favorite chili!

ingredients

1 cup low-fat milk

⅓ cup vegetable oil

1 egg

⅓ cup sugar

1 teaspoon kosher salt

1 cup yellow cornmeal

1 cup all-purpose flour

1 teaspoon baking soda

1 cup shredded Cheddar cheese

2 jalapeños, seeded, chopped

½ cup corn kernels

directions

1. Preheat oven to 350°F.

2. Lightly coat a 9 x 9 baking dish with cooking spray.

3. Using the dough attachment, place the milk, oil, and egg into the Food Processor Bowl. Turn unit ON and select MEDIUM. Blend until smooth.

4. Add the sugar, salt, cornmeal, flour, baking soda, cheese, jalapeño, and corn to the Food Processor Bowl and select MEDIUM. Blend until combined, scraping bowl as needed.

5. Pour the batter into the prepared baking dish.

6. Bake for 35–40 minutes or until a wooden pick inserted into the center comes out clean. Cool before serving.

1 SERVING: CALORIES 260; FAT 12G; SODIUM 410MG; CARBOHYDRATES 32G; SUGAR 9G; FIBER 1G; PROTEIN 7G

NINJA KNOW-HOW   USE LOW-FAT SHREDDED CHEDDAR AS AN EASY HEALTHY SWAP.

PREP TIME: 25 minutes   COOK TIME: 25 minutes   SERVINGS: 9   CONTAINER: 56-ounce Food Processor Bowl

cream cheese cinnamon sugar strudel

An easy recipe that can be made from scratch—use low-fat cream cheese as a healthy alternative.

ingredients

1 basic pie dough recipe, (recipe page 199)

1 package (8 ounces) low-fat cream cheese

1 teaspoon ground cinnamon

½ cup sugar

1 egg plus 1 tablespoon water, beaten

1 cup confectioners' sugar

2 tablespoons milk

directions

1. Take the pie dough out of the refrigerator 15 minutes prior to assembly.

2. Place the cream cheese, cinnamon, and sugar into the Food Processor Bowl. Turn unit ON and select MEDIUM. Blend until combined, scraping bowl as needed.

3. To assemble the strudels, place the pie dough on a lightly floured surface and roll both doughs into a 9 x 13 rectangle, about ⅛-inch thick. Cut each piece into thirds, which will form eighteen 3 x 4 rectangles.

4. Brush nine of the rectangles with egg wash and place a tablespoon of the filling in the middle of each rectangle, keeping a ½-inch border around it. Place a second rectangle on top and press all sides to seal. Cut slits into the tops of each filled rectangle with a small knife. Refrigerate for 30 minutes.

5. Preheat oven to 350°F.

6. Bake for 25 minutes or until golden brown. Cool. Combine confectioners' sugar and milk in a mixing bowl. Spread glaze on top of each strudel.

1 SERVING: CALORIES 290; FAT 12G; SODIUM 240MG; CARBOHYDRATES 40G; SUGAR 26G; FIBER 1G; PROTEIN 5G

 NINJA KNOW-HOW

EXPLORE DIFFERENT STRUDEL FILLINGS. TRY APPLES, ALMONDS, OR CHERRIES, OR EVEN SAVORY FILLNGS, LIKE PUMPKIN OR CARAMELIZED ONIONS.

PREP TIME: 15 minutes   COOK TIME: 15 minutes   RISE TIME: 1 hour   SERVINGS: 6   CONTAINER: 56-ounce Food Processor Bowl

soft pretzels

A brief dip in an alkaline water bath before baking gives pretzels their signature chewy crust. It also gives them their unique and indelible "pretzel" flavor.

ingredients

¾ cup warm water (110–115°F)

1 tablespoon sugar

1 package (¼ ounce) active dry yeast

1 teaspoon kosher salt

2¼ cups all-purpose flour

2 tablespoons unsalted butter, melted

Vegetable oil, for coating

⅔ cup baking soda

1 large egg yolk beaten with 1 tablespoon water

2 tablespoons kosher salt

directions

1. In a small bowl, place the water, sugar, and yeast. Allow to sit for 5 minutes.

2. Using the dough blade, place the yeast mixture, salt, flour, and butter into the Food Processor Bowl. Turn unit ON. Select LOW and blend for 15 seconds.

3. Remove the dough ball and place in a mixing bowl that has been coated with vegetable oil. Cover with plastic wrap and let sit in a warm place for 1 hour or until the dough has doubled in size.

4. Preheat the oven to 450°F. Line two half-sheet pans with parchment paper and lightly brush with the vegetable oil. Set aside.

5. Bring 10 cups of water and the baking soda to a boil in a saucepot.

6. Turn the dough out and divide into six equal pieces. Roll out each piece of dough into a 24-inch rope. Make a U-shape with the rope, holding the ends of the rope, then cross them over each other and press onto the bottom of the U in order to form the shape of a pretzel. Place onto the parchment-lined half-sheet pan.

7. Place the pretzels into the boiling water, one by one, for 30 seconds. Remove them from the water using a large flat spatula. Return to the half-sheet pan, brush the top of each pretzel with the beaten egg yolk and water mixture, and sprinkle with salt. Bake until dark golden brown in color, approximately 12–14 minutes. Transfer to a cooling rack for at least 5 minutes before serving.

1 SERVING: CALORIES 230; FAT 6G; SODIUM 2560MG; CARBOHYDRATES 38G; SUGAR 2G; FIBER 2G; PROTEIN 6G

NINJA KNOW-HOW

TRY SERVING PRETZELS WITH DIPPING SAUCES SUCH AS CHEESE, MUSTARD, PIZZA, OR CHOCOLATE.

PREP TIME: 20 minutes   COOK TIME: 30 minutes   SERVINGS: 12   CONTAINER: 56-ounce Food Processor Bowl

peach muffins

The combination of low-fat milk and nonfat yogurt gives these muffins the ultimate in moistness, with fewer calories!

ingredients

1¼ cups sliced peaches

1 teaspoon lemon juice

¼ cup vegetable oil

½ cup low-fat milk

¼ cup nonfat yogurt

2 teaspoons vanilla extract

1 large egg

¾ cup sugar

1¾ cups all-purpose flour

2 teaspoons baking powder

¼ cup ground flaxseeds

½ teaspoon kosher salt

directions

1. Preheat oven to 350°F. Lightly coat a 12-cup nonstick muffin pan with cooking spray. Place the peaches into the Food Processor Bowl. Turn unit ON. Hold down Auto-iQ™ PULSE until finely chopped. Remove peaches and set aside.

2. Using the dough attachment, place the lemon juice, oil, milk, yogurt, vanilla, and egg into the Food Processor Bowl. Turn unit ON. Select MEDIUM and blend until smooth.

3. Add the sugar, flour, baking powder, flaxseeds, salt, and chopped peaches. Select MEDIUM and blend until smooth, scraping bowl as needed.

4. Scoop the mixture into the prepared muffin pan, filling three-quarters full.

5. Bake for 30 minutes or until a wooden pick inserted into the center comes out clean. Cool before serving.

1 SERVING: CALORIES 190; FAT 7G; SODIUM 170MG; CARBOHYDRATES 31G; SUGAR 15G; FIBER 1G; PROTEIN 4G

NINJA
KNOW-HOW

BUY PEACHES AS RIPE AS POSSIBLE, PREFERABLY FROM A LOCAL SOURCE SUCH AS A FARMERS' MARKET.

PREP TIME: 1 hour   COOK TIME: 20–25 minutes   SERVINGS: 12   CONTAINER: 56-ounce Food Processor Bowl/Small 18-ounce Cup

greek pizza night

Make everything in your Ninja, dough sauce and toppings. Nothing beats homemade pizza from scratch.

ingredients

PIZZA DOUGH:

1 packet (¼ ounce) active dry yeast

1 teaspoon sugar

1¼ cups warm water (105–110*F)

4 cups all-purpose flour

1 teaspoon teaspoon salt

½ cup olive oil

Reserved flour

Reserved water

TOPPINGS:

sun-dried tomato sauce (page 122)

1½ cups low-fat mozzarella cheese

1 cup broccoli florets, fresh or frozen

1 cup thinly sliced red pepper

¼ cup sliced black olives

½ cup crumbled feta cheese

directions

1. FOR DOUGH: Combine the yeast, sugar, and warm water in a small bowl and set aside until foamy, about 5 minutes.

2. Using the dough attachment, place the flour, salt, olive oil, and the yeast mixture into the Food Processor Bowl. Turn unit ON and select LOW. Blend for 30 seconds until dough comes together. Remove the dough and form into two balls. Place one ball into a lightly oiled bowl. Cover loosely with plastic wrap and allow to rest and rise for 1 hour, until dough is doubled in size. Wrap the second ball in plastic wrap and freeze for up to 2 months.

3. Preheat oven to 375°F. Lightly spray a cookie sheet with nonstick spray and place the prepared pizza dough. Gently and evenly flatten out the dough all the way to the edges and ½ inch up the edge to form a crust.

4. Spoon the sun-dried tomato sauce, or your favorite pizza sauce evenly onto the dough, then top with mozzarella cheese, broccoli, red peppers, olives, and feta.

5. Bake for 20–25 minutes, checking halfway through, until crust is golden brown.

1 SERVING: CALORIES 310; FAT 14G; SODIUM 550MG; CARBOHYDRATES 36G; SUGAR 2G; FIBER 2G; PROTEIN 10G

NINJA KNOW-HOW USE HEALTHY VEGETABLES AND EVEN YOUR FAVORITE FRUIT FOR TOPPINGS TOO.

PREP TIME: 20 minutes   COOK TIME: 35 minutes   SERVINGS: 10–12   CONTAINER: 56-ounce Food Processor Bowl

coffee cake

This classic coffee cake is perfect for Sunday brunch, and easy to make.

ingredients

½ cup light brown sugar

¼ cup (½ stick) unsalted butter

¼ cup quick-cooking oats

½ teaspoon cinnamon

3 cups all-purpose flour, divided

¼ cup vegetable oil

½ cup low-fat milk

¼ cup low-fat sour cream

2 teaspoons vanilla extract

1 large egg

¾ cup sugar

2 teaspoons baking powder

½ teaspoon kosher salt

directions

1. Preheat oven to 350°F.

2. Lightly coat a 9 x 9 baking dish with cooking spray.

3. In a mixing bowl, combine the brown sugar, butter, oats, cinnamon, and 1 cup flour. Set aside.

4. Using the dough attachment, place the oil, milk, sour cream, vanilla, and egg into the Food Processor Bowl. Turn unit ON and select MEDIUM. Blend until smooth.

5. Add the sugar, 2 cups flour, baking powder, and salt to the Food Processor Bowl and hold down Auto-iQ™ PULSE until combined, scraping bowl as needed.

6. Pour the batter into the prepared baking dish. Spread the oat topping evenly on the batter.

7. Bake for 30–35 minutes or until a wooden pick inserted into the center comes out clean. Cool before serving.

1 SERVING: CALORIES 340; FAT 12G; SODIUM 200MG; CARBOHYDRATES 54G; SUGAR 23G; FIBER 1G; PROTEIN 5G

 NINJA KNOW-HOW   ADD ½ CUP BLUEBERRIES TO THE BATTER FOR AN ANTIOXIDANT BLAST.

PREP TIME: 15 minutes   COOK TIME: 9–12 minutes   SERVINGS: 48 cookies   CONTAINER: 56-ounce Food Processor Bowl

chocolate chip cookies

This will be the simplest way you will ever make cookies: all of the ingredients get blended in one bowl for easy prep and cleanup!

ingredients

2¼ cups all-purpose flour

1 teaspoon baking soda

1 teaspoon salt

2 sticks unsalted butter, softened

2 large eggs

1 teaspoon vanilla extract

¾ cup granulated sugar

¾ cup packed brown sugar

1½ cups Nestle Toll House semi-sweet chocolate morsels

directions

1. Preheat oven to 350°F. In a medium bowl, combine the flour, baking soda, and salt. Set aside.

2. Using the dough blades, add the softened butter, egg, vanilla, granulated sugar, and brown sugar to the Food Processor Bowl.

3. Turn unit ON and select LOW. Blend for 30 seconds, until creamed. Scrape down the sides.

4. Add the flour mixture to the Food Processor Bowl, then hold down Auto-iQ™ PULSE for 5 pulses. Remove the lid and scrape down the sides.

5. Select LOW and blend for another 30 seconds, until incorporated well.

6. Remove the dough blade and add the chocolate chips to the Food Processor Bowl. Using a wooden spoon, stir in the chocolate chips.

7. Drop the cookie batter by the tablespoon onto nonstick cookie trays, 2 inches apart. Bake for 9–12 minutes until golden brown.

1 SERVING: CALORIES 109; FAT 5G; SODIUM 176MG; CARBOHYDRATES 14G; SUGAR 9G; FIBER .5G; PROTEIN 1G

NINJA KNOW-HOW

ADD YOUR OWN SPIN BY ADDING WALNUTS, DRIED FRUIT, OR EVEN CINNAMON.

PREP TIME: 10 minutes   COOK TIME: 40 minutes   RISE TIME: 4 hours   SERVINGS: 8–10   CONTAINER: 56-ounce Food Processor Bowl

oatmeal raisin bread

A hearty artisan bread perfect for breakfast.

ingredients

¾ cup warm water
(110–115° F)

1 tablespoon sugar

1 package (¼ ounce) active
dry yeast

2 tablespoons vegetable oil

1 teaspoon kosher salt

1 cup unbleached bread flour

½ cup whole wheat flour

½ cup quick-cooking oats

1 cup dark raisins

directions

1. In a small bowl, place the water, sugar, and yeast. Allow to sit for 5 minutes.

2. Using the dough attachment, place the yeast mixture, oil, salt, flours, oats, and raisins into the Food Processor Bowl. Turn unit ON. Select LOW and blend for 15 seconds.

3. Remove the dough ball and place in a mixing bowl that has been coated with vegetable oil. Cover with plastic wrap and let sit in a warm place for 2 hours or until the dough has doubled in size.

4. Lightly coat a loaf pan with cooking spray. Form dough into a loaf and place in pan. Let rise for 2 hours or until double in size.

5. Preheat oven to 350°F.

6. Bake for 35–40 minutes or until golden brown. Cool before serving.

1 SERVING: CALORIES 190; FAT 4G; SODIUM 240MG; CARBOHYDRATES 36G; SUGAR 13G; FIBER 3G; PROTEIN 4G

NINJA
KNOW-HOW

WANT A SAVORY BREAD? INSTEAD OF RAISINS, ADD CHOPPED OLIVES AND ROSEMARY!

pie dough

A combination of butter and vegetable shortening creates the best consistency for the pie crust.

ingredients

2½ cups all-purpose flour

1 teaspoon kosher salt

6 tablespoons unsalted butter, cold, cut into cubes

5 tablespoons vegetable shortening baking stick, cold, cut into cubes

½ cup cold water

directions

1. Using the dough attachment, place the flour, salt, butter, and shortening into the Food Processor Bowl. Turn unit ON. Select MEDIUM and blend until combined.

2. Add the water and select Auto-iQ™ PULSE for 5 pulses.

3. Remove dough to a lightly floured work surface and knead to form a ball.

4. Divide dough into two pieces. Form each piece into a 1-inch-thick flattened disk. Wrap each piece with plastic wrap and refrigerate until needed.

1 SERVING: CALORIES 1200; FAT 71G; SODIUM 970MG; CARBOHYDRATES 119G; SUGAR 0G; FIBER 4G; PROTEIN 17G

NINJA KNOW-HOW   ALWAYS KEEP YOUR PIE CRUST AS COOL AS POSSIBLE. IN HOT WEATHER, MAKE YOUR PIE IN THE COOLER MORNING OR EVENING HOURS.

breads & baked goods

PREP TIME: 15 minutes   COOK TIME: 25 minutes   RISE TIME: 2 hours   SERVINGS: 12   CONTAINER: 56-ounce Food Processor Bowl

pizza dinner rolls

Turn pizza night into something more fun for the family.

ingredients

¾ cup warm water
(110–115°F F)

1 tablespoon sugar

1 package (¼ ounce) active
dry yeast

2 tablespoons vegetable oil

1 teaspoon kosher salt

1 tablespoon dried oregano

2 cups unbleached bread
flour

1 cup chopped fresh basil,
stems removed

½ cup pizza sauce

¾ cup shredded mozzarella
cheese

directions

1. In a small bowl, place the water, sugar, and yeast. Allow to sit for 5 minutes.

2. Using the dough attachment, place the yeast mixture, oil, salt, oregano, and flour into the Food Processor Bowl. Turn unit ON. Select LOW and blend for 15 seconds.

3. Remove the dough ball and place in a mixing bowl that has been coated with vegetable oil. Cover with plastic wrap and let sit in a warm place for 2 hours or until the dough has doubled in size.

4. Preheat oven to 350°F.

5. Lightly coat a 12-cup muffin pan with cooking spray. Divide the dough into 12 balls and then place in pan, pressing down in the center to create a deep well.

6. Fill well with basil and 1 teaspoon pizza sauce and top with 1 tablespoon mozzarella cheese on each.

7. Bake for 20–25 minutes or until golden brown.

1 SERVING: CALORIES 120; FAT 4.5G; SODIUM 250MG; CARBOHYDRATES 18G; SUGAR 2G; FIBER 1G; PROTEIN 5G

NINJA
KNOW-HOW

ADD DIFFERENT VEGETABLE FILLINGS SUCH AS SAUTEED ONIONS, BROCCOLI, AND MUSHROOMS TO CREATE A HEALTHIER MEAL.

PREP TIME: 15 minutes   COOK TIME: 15 minutes   SERVINGS: 10–12   CONTAINER: 56-ounce Food Processor Bowl

buttermilk biscuits

The Food Processor Bowl makes it so easy to make classic biscuits at home from scratch—prep and bake in 30 minutes! Serve biscuits with traditional chicken dinners or perfect for Sunday brunch!

ingredients

2 cups all-purpose flour

1 tablespoon baking powder

1 teaspoon baking soda

½ teaspoon kosher salt

2 teaspoons sugar

⅓ cup vegetable shortening baking stick, cold, cut into cubes

1 cup buttermilk

directions

1. Preheat oven to 425°F.

2. Using the dough attachment, place the flour, baking powder, baking soda, salt, and sugar into the Food Processor Bowl. Turn unit ON and select LOW. Blend for 5 seconds. Add the shortening and select LOW. Continue to blend until mixture resembles coarse crumbs.

3. Add buttermilk and hold down Auto-iQ™ PULSE until combined. Do not overmix.

4. Place the dough onto a lightly floured surface. Roll dough to ¾-inch thickness. Cut circles using a 2-inch round cutter. Press any scraps together using all the dough.

5. Place biscuits on a baking sheet lined with foil. Bake for 15 minutes.

1 SERVING: CALORIES 180; FAT 8G; SODIUM 380MG; CARBOHYDRATES 22G; SUGAR 2G; FIBER 1G; PROTEIN 3G

NINJA
KNOW-HOW

TRADITIONAL WITH FRIED CHICKEN AND GRAVY.

Lemon Bars, 213

CHAPTER 7:
dessert treats

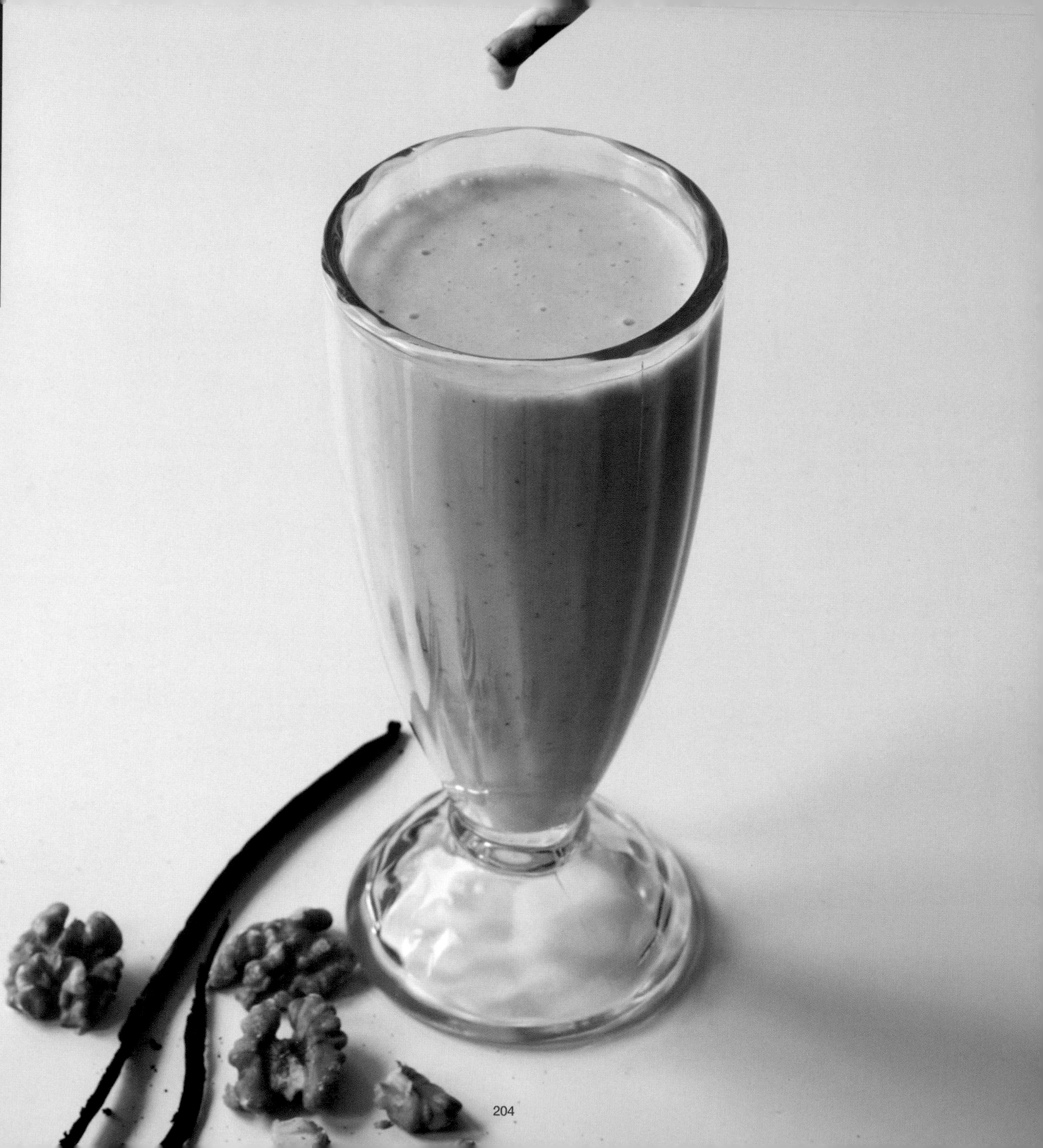

vanilla nut frozen treat

Prepare your own frozen dessert guilt-free! Add some fresh berries.

ingredients

⅓ cup vanilla oat milk

¼ cup walnut halves

¼ teaspoon pure vanilla extract

1 packet (.035 ounce) stevia

⅓ cup nonfat vanilla yogurt

1¼ cups ice

directions

1. Place all of the ingredients into the Small 18-ounce Cup in the order listed.

2. Turn unit ON, then select Auto-iQ™ Nutri Ninja® ULTRA BLEND.

1 SERVING: CALORIES 160; FAT 10G; SODIUM 50MG; CARBOHYDRATES 13G; SUGAR 10G; FIBER 1G; PROTEIN 5G

NINJA KNOW-HOW: YOU CAN SUBSTITUTE PECANS FOR THE WALNUTS FOR AN EVEN RICHER FLAVOR.

PREP TIME: 5 minutes SERVINGS: 1¼ cup CONTAINER: Small 18-ounce Cup

healthy dessert topping

It is so easy to make nut topping in your Nutri Ninja®.

ingredients

2 ounces 70% extra bitter cacao chocolate, chopped

1 cup walnut halves

½ teaspoon ground cinnamon

2 tablespoons light brown sugar

directions

1. Place all of the ingredients into the Small 18-ounce Cup.

2. Turn unit ON and hold Auto-iQ™ PULSE until desired chop.

1 SERVING: CALORIES 60; FAT 5G; SODIUM 0MG; CARBOHYDRATES 3G; SUGAR 2G; FIBER 1G; PROTEIN 1G

 NINJA KNOW-HOW | **TRY DIFFERENT NUTS FOR THIS TOPPING. PECANS, CASHEWS, MACADAMIA ARE REALLY GOOD.**

banana chocolate mousse

Bananas, avocado, chocolate, and orange combine in the decadent, delicious dessert.

ingredients

2 bananas, ripe, peeled, cut in quarters

2 avocados, ripe, peeled, pitted, cut in quarters

¼ cup chocolate syrup

½ orange, juiced

¼ cup cocoa powder

directions

1. Place all of the ingredients into the Food Processor Bowl. Turn unit ON and select MEDIUM. Blend until smooth, scraping down bowl as needed.

2. Place mousse into an airtight container and refrigerate until chilled.

1 SERVING: CALORIES 280; FAT 16G; SODIUM 25MG; CARBOHYDRATES 39G; SUGAR 19G; FIBER 11G; PROTEIN 4G

NINJA KNOW-HOW: REPLACE THE CHOCOLATE SYRUP WITH 2 OUNCES OF MELTED DARK CHOCOLATE IN THE MICROWAVE.

dessert treats

mango creamsicle

· ·

This is a really delicious recipe for a homemade yogurt dessert without all the calories of the commercial stuff

ingredients

1½ cups frozen mango

¼ cup coconut water

2 teaspoons honey

2 tablespoons nonfat yogurt

directions

1. Place all of the ingredients into the Small 18-ounce Cup in the order listed.

2. Turn unit ON, then select Auto-iQ™ Nutri Ninja® ULTRA BLEND.

1 SERVING: CALORIES 260; FAT 0G; SODIUM 25MG; CARBOHYDRATES 67G; SUGAR 59G; FIBER 6G; PROTEIN 4G

NINJA
KNOW-HOW

FOR A DELICIOUS VARIATION, SWAP FROZEN PEACHES FOR THE MANGO.

dessert treats

chocolate dipping sauce

• •

Chocolate dip is easy to make with your Nutri Ninja® Cup. Great for dipping strawberries or pouring over a bowl of raspberries.

ingredients

½ **cup water**

½ **cup agave nectar**

½ **teaspoon vanilla extract**

½ **cup cocoa powder**

⅓ **cup almond butter**

directions

1. Place all of the ingredients into the Small 18-ounce Cup.

2. Turn unit ON, then select Auto-iQ™ Nutri Ninja® BLEND.

1 SERVING: CALORIES 45; FAT 2G; SODIUM 10MG; CARBOHYDRATES 7G; SUGAR 6G; FIBER 1G; PROTEIN 1G

NINJA® KNOW-HOW | SWAP CASHEW BUTTER FOR ALMOND BUTTER AND ENJOY THE DIFFERENT TASTE.

PREP TIME: 20 minutes   COOK TIME: 30 minutes   SERVINGS: 10–12   CONTAINER: 56-ounce Food Processor Bowl

lemon bars

Everyone loves tangy lemon bars. These are easy to make with your Nutri Ninja® Food Processor Bowl.

ingredients

1 cup (2 sticks) unsalted butter, softened

2 cups sugar, divided

2⅓ cups all-purpose flour, divided

4 large eggs

⅔ cup freshly squeezed lemon juice

Confectioners' sugar to dust

directions

1. Preheat oven to 350°F.

2. Using the dough blade, place the butter, ½ cup sugar, and 2 cups flour into the Food Processor Bowl. Turn unit ON. Select MEDIUM and blend until smooth. Press crust into the bottom of an ungreased 9 x 13 baking dish. Bake for 15 minutes or until firm and golden in color. Cool for 10 minutes.

3. Place the eggs, 1½ cups sugar, ⅓ cup flour, and lemon juice into the Food Processor Bowl. Turn unit ON. Select MEDIUM and blend until smooth and sugar is dissolved. Pour mixture over the baked crust.

4. Bake for 20–23 minutes. They will firm as they cool.

5. Cool completely, and then dust with confectioners' sugar.

1 SERVING: CALORIES 460; FAT 21G; SODIUM 30MG; CARBOHYDRATES 64G; SUGAR 41G; FIBER 1G; PROTEIN 6G

NINJA KNOW-HOW — FOR PORTION CONTROL, CUT BARS INTO 20 SQUARES AND REDUCE THE CALORIES BY HALF.

dessert treats

lemon strawberry sorbet

It is so easy to make this almost instant sorbet with your Nutri Ninja® Cup.

ingredients

¾ **cup lemonade**

1½ **cups frozen strawberries**

directions

1. Place all of the ingredients into the Small 18-ounce Cup in the order listed.

2. Turn unit ON, then select Auto-iQ™ Nutri Ninja® ULTRA BLEND.

1 SERVING: CALORIES 160; FAT 0G; SODIUM 10MG; CARBOHYDRATES 42G; SUGAR 31G; FIBER 5G; PROTEIN 1G

NINJA®
KNOW-HOW
FOR A HEALTHY SWAP, SQUEEZE FRESH LEMON JUICE. ADD A BIT OF HONEY IF YOU WANT IT JUST A BIT SWEETER.

peach parfait

This delicious layered dessert will be a guaranteed five-star winner.

ingredients

2 cups heavy cream

2 cups sliced peaches

1 envelope (¼ ounce) unflavored gelatin

¼ cup water

2 tablespoons lemon juice

¾ cup sugar

3 cups chopped angel food cake

2 small bananas, sliced

1½ cups granola

directions

1. Place the heavy cream into the Food Processor Bowl. Turn unit ON. Select MEDIUM and blend until whipped, scraping sides as needed. Remove whipped cream to a mixing bowl and set aside.

2. Add peaches to the Food Processor Bowl. Turn unit ON. Select HIGH and blend until smooth.

3. Soak gelatin in cold water, then place into a saucepot, bring to a boil, and add the lemon juice and sugar, stirring occasionally to dissolve the sugar. Remove from heat and stir in peach puree.

4. Chill to room temperature, then fold in whipped cream. Refrigerate approximately 2 hours until set.

5. To serve, layer peach mousse, angel food cake, sliced banana, and granola in a parfait glass, repeating layers.

1 SERVING: CALORIES 366; FAT 11G; SODIUM 120MG; CARBOHYDRATES 43G; SUGAR 26G; FIBER 2G; PROTEIN 4G

NINJA KNOW-HOW FOR ADDED NUTRITION AND A TASTY TREAT, TOP WITH FINELY-CHOPPED DARK CHOCOLATE.

PREP TIME: 20 minutes COOK TIME: 1 hour SERVINGS: 10–12 CONTAINER: 56-ounce Food Processor Bowl

apple bundt cake

• •

This will be a favorite of all who taste it. Quick and easy in the Ninja Food Processor Bowl.

ingredients

4 green apples, peeled, diced

2 large eggs

1 cup plus 4 teaspoons sugar, divided

½ cup vegetable oil

⅓ cup orange juice

2 teaspoons vanilla extract

2 cups all-purpose flour

1 teaspoon baking powder

¼ teaspoon kosher salt

2 teaspoons ground cinnamon

directions

1. Preheat oven to 350°F. Grease a bundt pan with cooking spray.

2. Place diced apples in a strainer.

3. Using the dough attachment, place the eggs, 1 cup sugar, oil, orange juice, and vanilla into the Food Processor Bowl. Turn unit ON and select MEDIUM. Blend until smooth and sugar is dissolved.

4. Add the flour, baking powder, and salt to the Food Processor Bowl and select MEDIUM. Continue to blend until combined, scraping sides as needed.

5. Pour half of the batter into the prepared pan, then add a layer of apples and dust with 1 teaspoon cinnamon and 2 teaspoons sugar. Repeat with batter and apples. Bake for approximately 1 hour or until a knife inserted into cake comes out clean.

6. Let the cake cool for at least 1 hour before removing from pan.

1 SERVING: CALORIES 320; FAT 12G; SODIUM 105MG; CARBOHYDRATES 49G; SUGAR 28G; FIBER 2G; PROTEIN 4G

NINJA KNOW-HOW

DRIZZLE WITH THE CHOCOLATE DIPPING SAUCE FROM PAGE 212.

PREP TIME: 15 minutes **COOK TIME:** 45 minutes **SERVINGS:** 6 **CONTAINER:** 56-ounce Food Processor Bowl

pecan pie

Well worth the hour of prep and baking time. This is an extremely delicious easy-to-make version.

ingredients

½ cup sugar

¼ cup light brown sugar

¾ cup light corn syrup

4 tablespoons unsalted butter

3 large eggs

3 tablespoons spiced rum

1 teaspoon vanilla extract

¼ teaspoon kosher salt

1⅓ cups roughly chopped pecan halves

1 9-inch store-bought pie crust

directions

1. Place oven rack on bottom shelf.

2. Preheat oven to 325°F.

3. Place both sugars, corn syrup, and butter in a medium saucepot and cook over low heat, stirring constantly until sugar dissolves and butter melts. Remove from heat and cool to room temperature.

4. Place the cooled sugar mixture, eggs, rum, vanilla, and salt into the Food Processor Bowl. Turn unit ON. Select MEDIUM and blend until smooth.

5. Place the chopped pecans into the pie crust.

6. Pour filling into prepared pie crust and bake for 40–45 minutes or until pie is set. Let pie cool completely before serving.

1 SERVING: CALORIES 680; FAT 38G; SODIUM 310MG; CARBOHYDRATES 76G; SUGAR 57G; FIBER 2G; PROTEIN 7G

NINJA KNOW-HOW — CUT THE PIE INTO 12 PIECES AND CUT THE CALORIES IN HALF. IT WILL TASTE JUST AS GOOD.

PREP TIME: 15 minutes   COOK TIME: 20 minutes   SERVINGS: 12   CONTAINER: 56-ounce Food Processor Bowl

coconut cream cupcakes

When you are craving an expecially rich-tasting but relatively low-calorie cupcake, try this recipe. You will love it.

ingredients

½ cup vegetable oil

¼ cup whole milk

¾ cup water

1 teaspoon vanilla extract

1 package (16¼ ounces)
white cake mix

1 package (3.4 ounces)
coconut cream instant
pudding mix

4 large eggs

directions

1. Preheat oven to 350°F. Line a 12-cup muffin pan with cupcake liners.

2. Place all of the ingredients into the Food Processor Bowl. Turn unit ON and select MEDIUM. Blend until smooth, scraping sides as needed.

3. Scoop the mixture into the prepared muffin pan, filling three-quarters full.

4. Bake for 20 minutes or until a wooden pick inserted into the center comes out clean. Cool before serving.

1 SERVING: CALORIES 280; FAT 13G; SODIUM 380MG; CARBOHYDRATES 38G; SUGAR 22G; FIBER 1G; PROTEIN 4G

NINJA KNOW-HOW | TOP WITH YOUR FAVORITE FROSTING.

PREP TIME: 20 minutes   COOK TIME: 20 minutes   REFRIGERATE: 2 hours   SERVINGS: 8–10   CONTAINER: 56-ounce Food Processor Bowl

cannoli crepes

It's worth the effort to make your own cannoli crepes. The Ninja Food Processor Bowl makes it easy. Yummy!

ingredients

1 cup low-fat milk

3 large eggs

2 tablespoons melted unsalted butter

1 cup all-purpose flour

1 cup heavy whipping cream

1⅔ cups whole-milk ricotta cheese

1 cup powdered sugar

¼ teaspoon ground cinnamon

½ teaspoon vanilla extract

Zest ½ orange

½ cup semi-sweet mini chocolate chips

directions

1. Place the milk, eggs, butter, and flour into the Food Processor Bowl. Turn unit ON and select MEDIUM. Blend until smooth, scraping sides as needed.

2. Coat a nonstick sauté pan with cooking spray and heat over medium heat. Place a ¼ cup of the batter into the pan, tilting the pan with a circular motion so the batter coats the bottom evenly.

3. Cook for 1 minute or until the bottom is light brown. Turn and cook the other side. Set aside.

4. In a mixing bowl, whip heavy cream until there are stiff peaks.

5. In a separate mixing bowl, combine the ricotta cheese, sugar, cinnamon, vanilla, orange zest, and chocolate chips. Fold in the whipped cream. Refrigerate for 2 hours.

6. To serve, place one crepe on a plate and place ricotta mixture in the center. Roll to close.

1 SERVING: CALORIES 430; FAT 26G; SODIUM 95MG; CARBOHYDRATES 38G; SUGAR 22G; FIBER 1G; PROTEIN 12G

NINJA KNOW-HOW — SWAP THE MINI CHOCOLATE CHIPS FOR BUTTERSCOTCH CHIPS.

Lean Green Ninja, 45

index

index

index

Soups, Sauces & Entrées

NUTRI NINJA®

Nutri Ninja® | Ninja® Blender System
with Auto-iQ™ Technology

simply DELICIOUS,
simply NUTRITIOUS

150+ DELICIOUS RECIPES